Media
from Chaos to Clarity
and Back Again

*To the memory of Professor Don E. Schultz, the Father of IMC
and a generous mentor who always asked,
"What can I do for you?"*

*A steadfast believer in this work, you introduced its first two
editions with your words.
You are deeply missed and I will strive to honor your commitment
to asking the tough questions that move us closer to clarity.*

Media from Chaos to Clarity and Back Again

Third Edition

Judy Ungar Franks

Foreword by Charles Whitaker

BLOOMSBURY ACADEMIC
NEW YORK · LONDON · OXFORD · NEW DELHI · SYDNEY

BLOOMSBURY ACADEMIC
Bloomsbury Publishing Inc, 1359 Broadway, New York, NY 10018, USA
Bloomsbury Publishing Plc, 50 Bedford Square, London, WC1B 3DP, UK
Bloomsbury Publishing Ireland, 29 Earlsfort Terrace, Dublin 2, D02 AY28, Ireland

BLOOMSBURY, BLOOMSBURY ACADEMIC and the Diana logo are trademarks of
Bloomsbury Publishing Plc

First published in United States of America by the Marketing Democracy Ltd., 2011
This edition published 2026

Copyright © The Marketing Democracy Ltd., 2026

Cover design: Chloe Batch
Cover image © iStock/VLADGRIN

Bloomsbury Publishing Inc does not have any control over, or responsibility for, any
third-party websites referred to or in this book. All internet addresses given in this
book were correct at the time of going to press. The author and publisher regret any
inconvenience caused if addresses have changed or sites have ceased to exist, but can
accept no responsibility for any such changes.

A catalog record for this book is available from the Library of Congress.

ISBN: HB: 979-8-216-36738-3
PB: 979-8-216-36737-6
ePDF: 979-8-216-35143-6
eBook: 979-8-216-35142-9

Typeset by Newgen KnowledgeWorks Pvt. Ltd., Chennai, India
Printed and bound in the United States of America

For product safety related questions contact productsafety@bloomsbury.com.

To find out more about our authors and books visit www.bloomsbury.com
and sign up for our newsletters.

Contents

7 The Struggle for Clarity Continues   91

Part II And Back, Again: Welcome to Chaos Once More

8 The Fundamentals of the Media Business   105

9 Media as a Means to a Different End   119

Part III Clarity on the Horizon

Prelude: What to Expect in Part III

14 Fixing Media's Identity Crisis

15 Returning to the Essence of the Five Global Truths

16 Renewed Energy from the 3Cs

Epilogue   201

Foreword

Charles Whitaker

*Dean and Professor, Northwestern University, Medill School of
Journalism, Media, Integrated Marketing Communications*

These are disorienting and dispiriting times for those of us who came of age professionally in what some nostalgically call the golden era of media and advertising. Back in the so-called good old days, relationships reigned supreme. Editors knew their audiences intimately, publishers cultivated trust with advertisers, and the business itself was rooted in human connection, reinforced by the best available data at the time. Sure, stories of handshake deals over three-martini lunches have become lore, but those lunches represented something deeper: an era built on personal trust and shared understanding, not just transactions.

As a former magazine editor, I remember those halcyon days fondly. On the editorial side, our job was to nurture a connection with readers, creating content that resonated with their lives and interests. Meanwhile, our colleagues on the advertising sales side translated those relationships into demographic and psychographic profiles, promising advertisers an engaged and loyal audience. It wasn't perfect—the metrics were imprecise, and assumptions were often optimistic—but it worked. Dollars flowed, and everyone left the table feeling satisfied. But then, the world changed.

The arrival of digital disruptors in the late twentieth century was like a gale-force wind sweeping through an orderly marketplace. Big tech entered the fray with new platforms and technologies that promised precision. Algorithms could predict audience behavior; data could be mined to the last click. Suddenly, media no longer needed to rely solely on relationships or trust. Technology became the intermediary, redefining how audiences were reached and measured.

Executives from the old world—most of whom were clueless about the technology that had obliterated their business model—went scurrying to find ways to combat this scourge. But it is difficult to chart a new course for a ship that is battered and taking on water faster than the crew can bail it out. And the commanders of the SS Legacy Media were cast so adrift as the digital tsunami washed over them, that the vast majority floundered somewhat helplessly, incapable of seeing a clear path forward.

Times like these demand the perspective of someone who can rise above the fray, someone both steeped in the history of media and capable of seeing the opportunities that lie ahead. That someone is my colleague and friend, Judy Ungar Franks.

Judy, a professor at Northwestern University's Medill School of Journalism, Media, Integrated Marketing Communications, has devoted her career to helping us make sense of this messy media world. After nearly twenty-five years in the agency ranks at leading advertising and media firms—including Leo Burnett, Starcom, and Energy BBDO—Judy transitioned to academia in 2008. But she didn't merely bring her practical expertise to the classroom. She became a scholar of media transformation, dedicating her research to understanding the forces reshaping the industry.

When I first read *Media: From Chaos to Clarity* in its initial printing, I thought it was both insightful in its conceptualization of the changes that had battered media and prescient in its prescriptions for what was needed to address the downfall of so many media outlets and the outdated advertising practices that supported them. Judy delivered on her promise to provide clarity through the fog of digital disruption, but she didn't sugarcoat the message. Change was—and still is—needed, Judy declares. All of the hand-wringing about and tinkering around the edges of the old ways of doing business and wishing for better outcomes would not bring about a return to profitability. The world had changed dramatically, and all of us in media need to change with it.

Nearly fifteen years have passed since that first edition, and two editions later, Judy's message remains as important as ever. If anything, the world of media has become even more fractured and chaotic. The dominance of influencers as primary brand ambassadors, the shadowy hand of algorithms guiding consumer exposure and choices, and the manipulation and misrepresentation of content produced through generative AI pose all sorts of new issues one could barely have imagined nearly fifteen years ago. Yet Judy, with her conceptualization of the 3Cs of media—Channels,

Content, and Consumers—offers us an adaptable framework that helps us understand where we were and where we are headed on this media journey.

Which is not to suggest that Judy provides the panacea for all that ails modern media. But with the Five Global Truths as a compass, she offers clear and easy-to-digest principles that suggest how to remain current in a media environment that continues to change by the minute.

Judy doesn't just diagnose the problem; she also reminds us that not all is doom and gloom. Yes, the tools and rules have changed. Yes, the media landscape is different now. But the opportunity to thrive still exists—for those willing to adapt and embrace this new reality.

So, whether you're an old hand at media wondering what happened to the world you once knew or a digital native looking to make your mark, this book has something to offer. Judy Franks is here to guide you through the chaos—not with nostalgia for the past but with optimism for the future.

Acknowledgments

This third edition would not have come to life without the generous support and encouragement of many people, both new collaborators and longstanding champions of the work.

First, I would like to thank Dean Charles Whitaker and Associate Dean Vijay Viswanathan of the Medill School at Northwestern University for giving me the time and space to write. Their belief in this work—and in the importance of examining the media industry through an interdisciplinary lens—allowed this new edition to take shape.

A special thank you to Professor Scott Schiller of NYU Stern whose advocacy and insight pushed me to begin this third edition now, not later. Your encouragement made the difference.

I am grateful to Ashir Badami, head of Medill's Media Management and Leadership program, and to Professor Carolyn Tang Kmet of Medill's Integrated Marketing Communications (IMC) program for their careful review and thoughtful feedback. Thank you also to former graduate students Alex Gruhin and Julio Martín Velásquez for lending your insight and fresh perspective to the manuscript.

To Jeff Clennon, Senior Vice President (SVP) of Advertising and Partnerships at NBCUniversal, thank you for your honest reflections and deep understanding of the media landscape. And to Mike Moynihan, SVP of Brand, Marketing, Insights and Partnerships at the LEGO Group, thank you once again for your sharp eye, generous spirit, and thoughtful review.

A sincere thanks to Isabella Lima for her beautiful graphics that help bring the ideas in this book to life.

To Tracy Grant of the Leona Literary Agency, thank you for your wise counsel and for your friendship.

To the team at Rowman & Littlefield, now Bloomsbury Academic, thank you for your open-mindedness and commitment to publishing a book that refuses to be forced into any one mold. I'm grateful for your partnership and support.

To my students at Northwestern University, thank you for embracing this textbook. Your passion for a text that "reads like a good book" has inspired me to continue to write for you.

Finally, I would like to thank Steve and James. You know exactly what it means to share your life with someone who can't stop writing, rewriting, and editing just one more time. Your patience and love are present on every page, even when your names are not.

Disclaimer and Conditions of Use

This publication is intended for informational and educational purposes only. It provides general content designed to inform and provoke thoughtful engagement with the subject matter. While every effort has been made to ensure the accuracy and timeliness of the material as of the date of publication, the content is provided without warranties of any kind and should not be considered legal, financial, or professional advice.

The author and publisher disclaim any liability for loss, injury, or damages arising from the use of or reliance on the information presented. Any examples, references, or mentions of companies, technologies, platforms, or services are included for illustrative purposes only and do not constitute endorsements or recommendations.

No part of this publication may be reproduced, distributed, or transmitted in any form or by any means—electronic, mechanical, photocopying, recording, or otherwise—without prior written permission from the publisher, except as permitted under applicable copyright law.

The content of this publication may not be submitted to, ingested by, or used to train any generative artificial intelligence (AI) system, large language model (LLM), or machine learning application. This includes uploading content into automated tools or platforms designed to replicate, summarize, or reinterpret copyrighted works.

We appreciate your respect for the intended use and intellectual integrity of this work.

Introduction

Welcome to chaos. Here we are, in the throes of a media world that's fully digital—and very, very messy.

Before we jump in, I'd like to introduce myself and share a bit about our journey to date. If you've been along for the ride, welcome back. And if you're joining for the first time, don't worry. We'll get you caught up. Everything you need is right here.

Who Am I?

If we are going to spend some quality time together through the pages of this book, I owe you an introduction. An author should not just show up uninvited. My name is Judy Ungar Franks, and I am a professor at Northwestern University in Evanston, Illinois. I teach undergraduate and graduate media and consumer insight courses in the IMC degree programs at the Medill School of Journalism, Media, Integrated Marketing Communications.

I joined Northwestern University in 2008 following a twenty-three-year industry career where I rose to the executive ranks at Chicago's leading advertising and media services agencies, including Leo Burnett, FCB, Havas Chicago (formerly known as TLK), Starcom, and Energy BBDO. Today, I remain connected to the agency community by serving as an instructional designer and facilitator for the 4A's (American Association of Advertising Agencies) Learning Institute, where I designed and currently facilitate two courses: Marketing Essentials and Media Essentials.

I believe the best learning happens at the intersection of theory and practice, and my past experiences working on brands such as P&G, Hallmark, Allstate, Wrigley, and LEGO, among others, helped shape how I view the media world today. However, the media world today looks very different from the world I experienced firsthand in my agency career. In order to teach modern media, you have to study it! Media is constantly changing, and my research has taken me on a journey to explore many topics, such as binge viewing, audience attention distribution across media economic forms, programmatic advertising, and recently, how advertising experiences can be a friend, a foe, or a frenemy to healthy media–audience relationships.

I believe that media is best understood at the intersection of timeless principles and timely applications. You can't figure out where to go if you don't know where you've been! That's why at this stage of my career I am dedicated to updating this "little book that could" to provide a timeline and to fill in some of the gaps in our collective knowledge.

Who Are You?

Perhaps you picked up this book because you heard it was "a good read" that offers an insightful view of today's messy media world. Or perhaps it was assigned to you as required reading, and you had no choice! Regardless of your reason for opening the book, I assure you that our conversation will be time well spent, as we aim to provide clarity in a field that often feels chaotic.

Whether you've been around for a long time and are scratching your head wondering what happened to a media world that used to make sense, or you grew up in this crazy media world that seems perfectly normal to you, this book is for you. The book aims to explain the media world in a way that situates the present with the past so that you can better understand where we've been to help determine where we're going. We'll provide the big picture to help you see beyond all the shiny objects and the sound bites that can cloud your view. Our goal is to provide some clarity—if the media themselves cooperate! It's quite messy out there.

What you do with this insight is up to you. Some of you will use the book to help transform media companies that have lost their way. Others will develop more engaging marketing strategies for brands. Still others will build new models for journalism to thrive for all members of society. And some will use this book to help them pass a final exam! This book is for everyone. It doesn't take a side or hold any particular bias.

Why Did I Write This Book in the First Place?

To fully understand the motivation behind this book, we need to go back to 2008 when I was transitioning from the agency world to academia. The iPhone was only one year old, and the media landscape was clearly shifting, but no one knew how to talk about it effectively. There were two extreme viewpoints: one suggested that the sky was falling and analog media would be obliterated by digital, while the other saw digital media as just an additional channel to be integrated into the existing business model.

I believed there was a more nuanced explanation waiting to be discovered and discussed. To find it, we needed to move beyond sensational headlines and study the underlying dynamics of what was truly happening. This book was conceived as a means to delve into those complexities, offering a deeper understanding of the evolving media landscape. By examining the transition from analog to digital media, we aimed to provide a compass to navigate this evolution effectively.

Our Journey So Far

The first edition of *Media: From Chaos to Clarity* was published back in 2011. In this edition, we aimed to establish some semblance of a coherent conversation around the evolution of the media world from analog to digital. We introduced the Five Global Truths that could be used as a compass to navigate the chaos. We celebrated the pioneers who led us to each truth and introduced a new energy formula, the 3Cs, for explaining the relationship between Content, Consumers, and Channels (Franks 2011).

The second edition of the book was written in 2017 and published at the beginning of 2018—a little over ten years after the launch of the iPhone. This anniversary served as an appropriate milestone to reevaluate whether the Five Global Truths still held relevance in the rapidly evolving digital age. Were we right? Or did any of the Truths collapse? By analyzing the media landscape at this point in time, we found that not only did they hold up, but they also became even more relevant. The second edition provided updated research and real-world examples to illustrate how these Truths had manifested in the modern media landscape. This edition reaffirmed the validity of the original insights while expanding the discussion to encompass new developments and challenges that lie ahead.

Moreover, the 3Cs energy formula that was originally introduced in the first edition still seemed right for the times—the media ecosystem thrived on content that could touch the heads and hearts of consumers who then used conveniently accessible channels to accelerate content at the speed of share.

What's in Store?

With more time under our belts, it became necessary to revisit the media landscape with a critical eye. Are the Five Global Truths still holding up? Maybe. But maybe not. The evolution of digital media has accelerated into something far more complex, with powerful new players and shifting audience behaviors reshaping the field in real time.

This book is designed to help make sense of that complexity. Rather than diving deep into one particular channel or pocket of the ecosystem, we'll zoom out to see the full picture—connecting the dots between historical shifts, business models, audience behaviors, and emerging technologies. We'll explore how the pieces fit together so we can better understand where things stand now and where they might be headed next.

The structure of the book reflects that journey: Part I grounds us in the forces that shaped the digital media landscape we live in today. Part II unravels all the complexities of the media business today. Part III asks what comes next, offering strategic insights to help chart a more purposeful path forward.

You don't need to have read the previous editions to find your footing. We'll revisit foundational ideas like the Five Global Truths and the 3Cs energy formula and bring everyone into the conversation as we go.

The book is written in a style that aims to feel more like a conversation than a lecture. It is designed for curious learners of all types—whether you're new to media, working inside the business, or simply trying to make sense of what's happening around you. Complex ideas will be covered with clarity and purpose, without being oversimplified. And throughout, we'll prioritize integrated thinking: how technologies, business models, and cultural shifts work together—not in isolation—to shape the media world we experience every day.

Whatever brings you here, the goal is the same: to offer clarity in a media environment that often feels overwhelming.

No Overpromises Here

You'll notice a slight shift in the title: *Media from Chaos to Clarity and Back Again*! We are at a unique point in time that's looking rather messy and complex. We may not have all the answers this time around, but we will put all the issues on the table. The Five Global Truths got us to where we need to be. Now, it's up to us to forge the pathway ahead.

I look forward to sharing this thinking with you in the coming chapters. You may not agree with every point nor will every suggested action be relevant to you. But I hope you will be inspired to view the messy media world in a new light and that the ideas in this book will help you thrive in your pursuits.

Best wishes,
Judy Ungar Franks

Part I

Media from Chaos to Clarity

Prelude: What to Expect in Part I

Part I takes us back to where the story began—when chaos first took hold as digital technology disrupted the rules of the media game. But this section isn't just a history lesson. It's a guided journey through media time, designed to show you how the analog media world operated with a sense of order, and what happened when that order began to unravel.

We'll start by redefining what media actually is—not just the channels but also the content that fills them and the consumers whose attention gives media its value. In Chapter 1, we establish this more expansive definition rooted in the 3Cs: Content, Channels, and Consumers.

Chapter 2 walks us through the journey from analog to digital, helping new readers get caught up and returning readers see the continuity of this transformation. It ends with a provocative question: Was the clarity we once gained ever really permanent?

Chapter 3 introduces the Five Global Truths, which first emerged in earlier editions of this book. These truths continue to hold explanatory power in today's digital landscape, and you'll see how they operate as a compass in the midst of change.

Chapter 4 expands the cast of characters. We examine the new players who now call themselves media—from creators and platforms to marketers and retailers—all competing for consumer attention and redefining the media ecosystem.

Chapter 5 explores the rise of platforms as the new power brokers. These aren't just facilitators of content—they are infrastructure owners, data miners, and distribution gatekeepers who now dominate the business of media.

Chapter 6 looks at the rise of first-party audience data and how it's reshaping the economics of media. As third-party cookies face ongoing scrutiny and regulatory pressure, the ability to collect and activate first-party data has become a central source of strategic advantage. The chapter ends with an open question: Is data becoming more valuable than content itself?

Finally, Chapter 7 reminds us that the evolution of media is never complete. Just as we begin to find clarity, new forces emerge. The chapter challenges us to separate true transformation from short-lived distractions and to consider how audiences across generations adapt—or resist—as innovation continues to unfold.

Together, these chapters provide the timeline, tools, and context needed to understand our travels toward the world we live in today. We have arrived in a fully digital media landscape. And while that chapter closes, new challenges lie ahead.

What Is Media?

Media. It's a term we all use, but rarely do we stop to define it. As we dive into this book, we must first agree on what we're talking about when we use the term "media." Without this common understanding, any discussion about its evolution, impact, or future becomes muddled.

Media are channels, right? Sure, they are. Channels are an integral part of the equation. They represent the communication technologies that connect senders with receivers. And for a long time, they were the stars of the story. You turned on the TV to watch, picked up the phone to talk, and opened the newspaper to read. You used your computer to search. You get the gist. A focus on channels as a proxy for the broader concept of media was simple and direct.

But today, that definition doesn't go far enough.

A New Definition

For our purposes, media is best understood as the interrelationship among three essential forces—what we'll refer to throughout this book as the 3Cs:

- Channels: communication technologies and interfaces that deliver media experiences from sender to receiver(s).

- Content: the messages and material that flow through those channels—created to entertain, inform, or persuade.
- Consumers: the individuals, communities, and/or masses who receive and interpret the media experience. Their attention is what powers the entire media economy.

Media Defined
Media is the Interrelationship Among the 3Cs

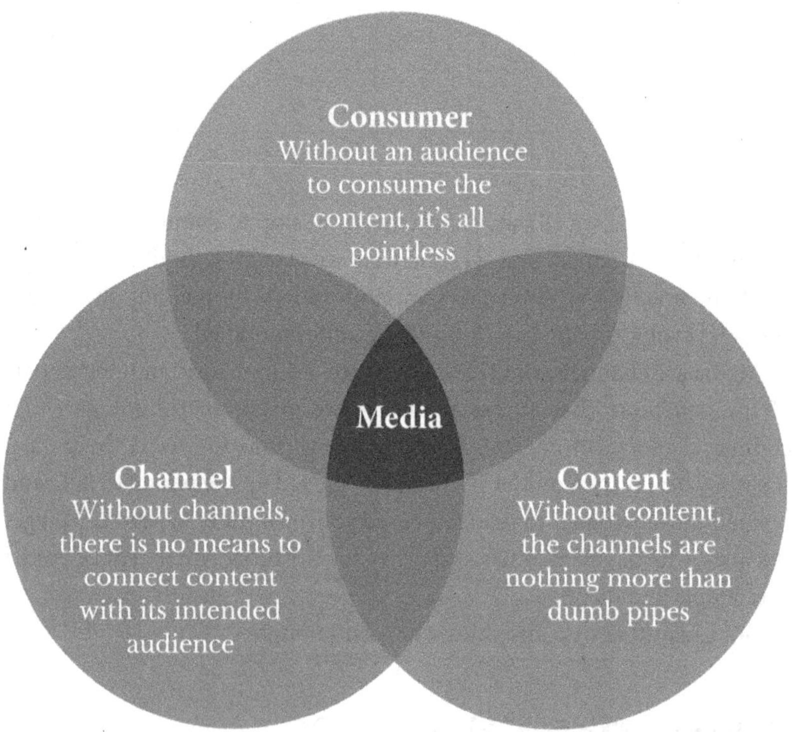

This expanded definition may very well be the key that unlocks the rest of this book.

Once digital came onto the scene, a media narrative that had long centered on channels—what we used, when we used it, and why—gave way to something far more complex. Channels started to blend and overlap. Content became unbound from its original formats. And audiences stepped forward not just to receive media, but to choose it, curate it, share it and even create it.

To understand media today, we believe it must be studied as a living system where the interaction among Channels, Content, and Consumers gives rise to value, meaning, and influence.

But it didn't used to be this way. To understand where we are now, we have to start at the beginning. Not the beginning of time per se; but we have to rewind to a time when the media world was mainly analog.

When Channels Were the Story

Once upon a time, a focus on channels alone was enough. Why? Because channels weren't just how media got delivered—they *were* the media experience.

We waited for the phone to ring—hoped it would ring—and when it finally did, we'd drag that coiled cord as far as it would stretch, into the hallway or behind a door, carving out a few moments of private conversation in a shared house. That moment was the medium.

On Saturday nights, we gathered around the television—not just to watch, but to *be together* in the watching. The clock dictated the show; the network dictated the schedule. If you missed it, you missed it. That was the deal. That structure brought us together, built anticipation, and created a sense of occasion.

These weren't just communication tools. They were cultural rituals. Watching wasn't just a verb; it was an event. Reading the Sunday paper wasn't just staying informed; it was a shared routine passed from hand to hand, section to section.

And then the first-generation digital era arrived.

We got our first desktop computer, usually in the family room. You'd click the big blue "E," wait for the dial-up tone to finish its robotic song, and then—just maybe—you'd connect to the internet. Accessing a webpage felt like stepping through a portal. Even email was a moment. "You've got mail" wasn't just a notification; it was a thrill.

Early texting was its own revolution. If you had a mobile phone that could send an SMS, you were ahead of the curve. You learned to tap the number keys just right to spell out your thoughts, and doing it well made you feel connected, modern—even cool.

In every case, the channel experience itself was still unique. Even in the earliest digital days, the novelty *was* the medium.

Channels didn't just transmit content. They shaped our relationships, our routines, and even our sense of time. And each one had its own language: radio spoke in voices, print in columns, television in moving pictures, early internet in loading bars and link blue, and billboards in bold proclamations you saw at 55 miles per hour.

For a long time, that was enough. Channels were the central part of the story because each was unique in terms of its communication technology, content format, and service to the audience.

Channels gave media its meaning.

Channels Evolve with Advances in Communication Technology

It would be convenient to say that "digital transformation" changed everything. But the reality is more nuanced. Digital didn't arrive and instantly redefine media. It began as just another channel. Something you accessed through a desktop computer, a dial-up modem, or maybe an early mobile phone. It had its own quirks and limitations, just like print, radio, or television.

The real shift began when digital stopped being a separate track and started to infiltrate every other mode of communication. As content became digitized and as more channels became digitally compatible, the distinctions between channels began to dissolve. Now, the same video, article, or conversation can travel across any device, any screen, anytime.

Today, it all boils down to which screen you choose to use—your computer, your tablet, your smart TV, or your mobile phone. They're all capable of delivering the same content to the same audience.

Audiences have adapted accordingly. Convenience rules. People move fluidly among devices, choosing whatever's most accessible at the moment.

In the coming chapters of this book, we will take you on a journey through media time to give you the full story. But for now, we need to focus our attention on the fact that channels themselves morph and mutate with advances in technology. The evolution of communication technology is a fascinating story, but it isn't the full story.

Channels without Content Are Nothing More than Dumb Pipes

In today's digital media world, the lines between media and technology have blurred. Where does true media start and stop? What about the digital technologies that function like utilities in our daily lives? Is Google a platform, an aggregator, or a form of media? What about Facebook and X (formerly known as Twitter)? Are they dumb pipes that carry our social conversations? Or are they forms of media?

A primary distinction between media and communication technologies is the responsibility for the content they carry. Media companies hold responsibility for the content they produce and/or distribute. Yet, communication technologies get a free pass. Section 230 of the Communications Decency Act enables communication technologies to enact community standards for content that is carried on their platforms while also granting these technologies immunity from any liability for said content (47 U.S.C. § 230 1996). Communication technologies can weave in and out of the media conversation when it's convenient for them. When it comes to monetizing their platforms, they certainly want to be part of the media ecosystem to garner their fair share of advertising revenue. Yet, when their algorithms manipulate outcomes and lead audiences and/or advertisers to egregious content, the same companies plead innocence and immunity from any responsibility for the content they carry.

Content is a key ingredient. A channel without content—whether you assume responsibility for it or not—is nothing more than a dumb pipe. Yes, that's a real term.

Channels and Content Need an Audience

As our definition of media expands to include both channels and content, we have a clearer picture; yet it isn't fully complete. Media ultimately thrives on the attention of audiences who act as consumers of content. Without an audience, it's all pointless.

Professor Philip Napoli (2003) explained this phenomenon as the Dual Product Marketplace. Media produce and/or distribute content (product one) that attracts the attention of audiences who consume the content (product two). He also explained that audiences have the autonomy to select media that suits their wants, needs, and interests (Napoli 2003).

In today's digital age, we have more content than we can consume, relatively easy access to the channels that distribute the content, and only a fixed amount of attention to go around. That's why the integration of the audience as consumers of content is crucial.

Media's 3Cs: Channels, Content, and Consumers

When you put all the pieces together, you can see that media is more than the sum of its parts. It's the entire ecosystem that supports the creation, distribution, and consumption of content. It involves communication technology (i.e., channels), the content distributed across these channels, and the consumers who ultimately engage with the content. In essence, it's the intersection of three Cs: Channels, Content, and Consumers. This comprehensive definition acknowledges that without the channel, content cannot reach its audience; without content, a channel is just a dumb pipe; and without an audience, neither content nor channel holds value. Each is important on its own, but the real story lies in the relationship among these "three Cs" and how they influence each other.

In the coming chapters, we'll use this definition as our foundation. We'll explore how communication technologies and content formats have evolved, how we relate to it as individuals, as members of our communities and in culture, and how we can navigate an ever-changing ecosystem with its host of new players. But first, we needed to establish this baseline understanding. With a clear definition in hand, we're ready to delve into the chaos and clarity of the media world.

2

The Journey through Media Time

Once upon a time and not all that long ago, we lived in a very different media world that we affectionately coined the Newtonian Media World. From the 1950s, when television came of age in the United States, all the way toward the end of the twentieth century, this mainly analog media world functioned like a predictable, well-oiled machine. The media systems were relatively stable, and each major form of media had unique characteristics and specific benefits. It was an era of absolutes. Once you understood how a particular media channel worked, you could count on it to function with a high degree of consistency.

This Newtonian Media Era was defined by a dominant set of media forms: a small handful of national broadcast television networks, AM radio stations with broad reach in each local market (later joined by FM), and metropolitan daily newspapers that served as the primary sources of news and information. Billboards along main roads and highways were visible to nearly everyone, and magazines—though targeted by interest areas, from newsweeklies to women's lifestyle titles—still circulated widely. The household television set stood as the centerpiece of the living room. These channels commanded mass audiences and largely dictated what people watched, read, saw, and listened to each day.

Some of you might remember this media world firsthand. Others may have come of age during the messy transition period when that world was beginning to change. And for some of you, it's a relic you've only heard about from others. Regardless of whether you personally experienced this era or your media life has always been digital, revisiting this history matters. You need the backstory to understand how today's digital media landscape functions. Because nearly everything we now take for granted works the opposite of how it used to.

Most people refer to this past media era as the "analog" media era and/or the "mass" media era. And it's a good place to start. At the time, media capacity was relatively limited. There were technical limitations on how many analog media channels could fit on the electromagnetic spectrum. And given the overhead costs to print and distribute paper-based media, the options were relatively constrained there as well. There were far fewer choices for how audiences could spend their time with media, and as a result, each form of media could attract mass audiences.

While the terms "analog" and "mass" are helpful descriptors, they don't go quite far enough in explaining why the media world functioned in such a predictable manner. To truly understand it, we need to look under the hood. What made this media system so stable, so consistent, and so powerful for so long?

We took apart the metaphorical media machine to better understand how it operated. From this dissection, five defining characteristics emerged. These were broad patterns that held true across most media forms and time periods, even as exceptions and competitive dynamics existed within the system.

> *Certainty*: Every media channel had a defined function and utility, with limited overlap. Audiences fit these different media into their repertoire based on the unique benefits each one provided. While individual channels certainly competed with each other, sometimes fiercely, their operating structures, business models, and audience behaviors remained relatively stable and predictable.
>
> *Selection*: Audiences gravitated toward media forms that suited them best. Heavy users of one media form often consumed less of another. That didn't mean people used only one kind of media; but they did develop clear favorites, and their habits were more segmented by media type than they are today.
>
> *Linear*: Content moved from Point A to Point B in largely uninterrupted fashion. Communication flowed primarily one way—from sender to

receiver—and usually from one to many. If someone wanted to share some form of content, the act required effort and rarely extended beyond a small circle.

Functional: Each media channel had its own technical and operational requirements that shaped both content and consumption. Everything from content formats to audience measurement protocols was specific to that channel, reinforcing its distinct identity and role in the ecosystem.

Channel-centric: Because there were relatively few media outlets, channels themselves could attract and hold mass audiences. They maintained "audience flow" across full schedules of programming, becoming the economic engines of the media business in the process.

These five characteristics weren't absolutes, nor were they mutually exclusive. But together, they defined the Newtonian Media World—a term borrowed from science, where systems were structured, predictable, and governed by fixed laws. It was a media era grounded in stability, clarity, and control—the very conditions that made the system understandable and its patterns relatively predictable.

This structured system didn't just shape the media channels; it created the conditions in which each of the 3Cs of media functioned in consistent and clearly defined ways. The mechanics of the system made it possible for the entire media ecosystem to follow a set rhythm, giving each "C" a stable role to play.

Channels held power and control. They programmed content, reached audiences directly, and monetized attention through advertising and/or subscriptions. Channels operated with near-complete control over distribution and access, cementing their position as economic linchpins.

Content was structured and scheduled. Editorial decisions followed journalistic norms and programming grids. Content creation followed fixed production cycles—daily papers, weekly magazines, seasonal TV schedules—creating a rhythm that aligned with consumption.

Consumers followed well-defined patterns. Morning routines included newspaper reading, midday might bring drive-time radio, and evenings centered around network television. Measurement tools were built to track these habits on a fixed schedule.

The Media Business in the Newtonian Era

The business model in this era was also straightforward: most media companies operated in a dual product marketplace (Napoli 2003). They produced content for audiences and sold audience attention to advertisers. There was clarity in how value was created and exchanged. Scarcity created demand. High barriers to entry (e.g., printing presses and FCC (Federal Communications Commission) licenses) limited competition and preserved profits. Audiences paid with their time and/or with money. And most media companies were richly rewarded. It was a stable economic system built on scarcity, scale, and predictability.

The Newtonian Machine Started to Break Down

Toward the end of the twentieth century, legacy media began to evolve. Cable television emerged with dozens of new channels targeting increasingly specific interests. FM radio overtook AM for music listening and splintered into narrowly focused formats. Satellite radio entered the mix and created even more choices. Magazines proliferated across every imaginable niche. Local newspapers faced national competition. Media, once concentrated, began to fragment. Scarcity gave way to abundance.

The proliferation of channels became a catalyst that reshaped the dynamic among the 3Cs in profound ways. Just as the Newtonian Media World accommodated the 3Cs—Channels, Content, and Consumers—with structure and predictability, this emerging period of media evolution began to unravel that order. What had once been a tightly organized, top-down system started to loosen, introducing greater choice, more specialization, and less control across the media landscape.

Channels became fragmented. What was once a consolidated lineup of dominant outlets fractured into dozens, then hundreds, of competing voices. It became increasingly difficult for any single outlet to scale a mass audience the way legacy channels once could.

Content diversified within established formats. While some content still commanded broad attention—such as network TV finales, major news events, and live sports—there was a growing volume of specialized content that could serve niche tastes. Content diversification became the norm across every media form.

Consumers exhibited unprecedented autonomy. Rather than sticking to familiar routines shaped by a few dominant outlets, audiences began traversing a wider range of options. They no longer had to settle for generalized programming; they could seek out content that more precisely matched their tastes, preferences, and interests. Media habits became more individualized, disrupting the predictability that once defined audience behavior.

The media system was no longer one of certainty but one of experimentation and paradox. Suddenly, mass and niche media coexisted and the traditional rules of mass media were no longer sufficient to explain audience behavior. The Newtonian machine hadn't collapsed, but cracks were forming in its once-stable foundation.

The Media Business under Strain

Even as media companies continued to operate within the familiar dual product paradigm—creating content to attract audiences, then selling that audience attention to advertisers—the system was beginning to feel pressure. The audience, once concentrated within a few reliable channels, was now scattering across a growing number of options. Those in search of attention—marketers, publishers, programmers—had to follow. Cross-channel strategies became essential, not just to grow reach, but to hold onto it.

This period also marked a subtle but important shift in where value was perceived to reside. Channels had long served as proxies for audience scale. But as fragmentation increased, it became clear that content itself—when relevant, compelling, or entertaining enough—could pull audiences across platforms. While channels still played a critical role in distribution and reach, they could no longer rely on their position alone. Attention had to be earned—and great content mattered more than ever.

Making Digital Fit

Then came something entirely new: digital media. In its earliest form, it was confined to desktop computers. Websites were static. Search engines were rudimentary. The internet was slow. At first, the industry tried to treat digital like just another communication technology—one that could be absorbed into the existing media system. We borrowed familiar terms to describe the unfamiliar. Early display ads were called "billboards" and "banners." Website traffic was counted like foot traffic past a storefront. These analogies now seem simplistic, but they helped us make sense of the new environment by relating it back to the systems we already knew.

In its first stage, the digital media business was built almost entirely on advertising. The advertising model took a page from what was known as "direct response" advertising in the Newtonian Media World. It was relatively low risk. You pay for performance. In this case, a "click."

This approach seemed reasonable—for a while. As long as digital was used primarily for search and information retrieval, it didn't disrupt the Newtonian machine too severely. Digital could be managed as a parallel ecosystem that ran alongside the analog channels that everyone knew so well.

But digital media didn't stay in that lane. Its growing capacity to create, distribute, and monetize content eventually overwhelmed the old framework. What once seemed like a supplemental tool became the catalyst for a much larger upheaval. Digital wasn't just another channel; it was a capacity-expanding force. The strain that had been building within the Newtonian Media World became harder to contain, and its orderly mechanics began to break apart.

The Moment Everything Changed

That tipping point arrived with the launch of the iPhone in 2007. While BlackBerry and others had introduced smartphones earlier—some with internet browsing and messaging capabilities—Apple redefined the category. It offered not only sleek design and functionality but also a fully integrated ecosystem, complete with the App Store, which transformed the phone into a customizable hub for every form of media. Suddenly, the internet was in our pockets, and every facet of our lives could be mediated through a single screen.

Once digital escaped the confines of desktop computers and became mobile, the cracks in the old system widened into fractures. The media world we once knew—already under strain—began to break apart at an accelerated pace. Media of every kind evolved in ways we hadn't seen before. It was messy. The familiar laws that had governed the Newtonian Media World no longer applied. The orderly, stable system gave way to something unpredictable and unruly. Welcome to chaos.

Yet human beings aren't hardwired to deal with chaos. We like to know what to expect. We crave a sense of order. In our quest for that order, we developed coping mechanisms to make sense of this digital disruption. But many of these frameworks fell short or created new complications:

> *The Apocalypse Theory*: The belief that new digital media would destroy old analog media entirely. The truth? Media doesn't die unless it's weak to begin with.
>
> *What Is Past Is Prologue*: The belief that we could integrate digital media into legacy systems using old playbooks. But transformation on this scale required new thinking.
>
> *Carpe Technology Diem*: The tendency to chase every new technology as the savior of media. Yet technology is only one part of the media equation—alongside audience and content.

At this point, we were no longer dealing with a mere evolution in media. We were experiencing something more profound. We had fully entered a digital media world in all its complexity. Channels had changed, content creation and consumption had changed, and audience behavior had fundamentally shifted.

In order to explain what we were seeing, we needed a new way to talk about media evolution. That's why we built a compass to guide the way. In the next chapter, we'll introduce and unpack the Five Global Truths that have served as a reliable compass. They explained our journey from the analog to the digital media world, and we'll test their utility in guiding us further.

Here We Are Today

But before we move on, we need to acknowledge where we are today. Things certainly move quickly. And the digital tipping point that took place with the launch of the iPhone not even twenty years ago is definitely in the rearview mirror. Today, we are living in a fully digital media world that barely resembles what came before. The predictability of the Newtonian system is gone. The transitional era is behind us. The rules, the players, and the business models have all changed. Today's digital world is more niche than it is mass. It's complicated and filled with players who aren't necessarily fully committed to the 3Cs of media. It's dominated by platforms with value tied to consumer actions and commerce. It's why we're here and what we will unpack throughout this book.

But before moving on, it may help to summarize history in one simple table. The table below summarizes the key shifts in mindset, business model, and the 3Cs of media across four distinct phases in media's evolution.

The Journey Through Media Time: Summary Table
Understanding the Shifting Logic Behind Media's Past and Present

	Newtonian Media Era (1950s–1990s)	Analog Media Fragmentation Era (1990s–early 2000s)	Digital Tipping Point (2007–late 2010s)	Modern Digital Era (late 2010s–present)
Defining Characteristics				
Mass vs. Niche	Mass	Mass and Niche	Mass Declining, Niche Rising	Mass Declining, Niche Rising
Analog vs. Digital	Analog	Analog with Emerging Digital	Analog and Digital Begin to Converge	Fully Digital
Defining Mindset	Certainty and Control	Autonomy and Signs of Stress	Disruption and Need for New Logic	Complexity and Competing Interests
Primary Business Model	Dual Product Marketplace: Both Content and Audience Attention Drive Economic Value	Dual Product Marketplace: Fragmentation Puts Stress on the Model	Dual Product Marketplace: Digital Adopts Direct Response Ad Model	Multi-Sided Platform Model: Value Tied to Actions and Commerce

The Journey Through Media Time: Summary Table
Understanding the Shifting Logic Behind Media's Past and Present

The 3Cs	Newtonian Media Era (1950s–1990s)	Analog Media Fragmentation Era (1990s–early 2000s)	Digital Tipping Point (2007–late 2010s)	Modern Digital Era (late 2010s–present)
Consumer	Stable and Predictable Media Repertoires	Growing Autonomy: Media Repertoires Less Stable and Predictable	Accelerated Choice and Agency: Media Repertoires Become Mobile and Social	Hyper-Individualized: Media Repertoires Shaped By Personal Preferences and Algorithms
Content	Professionally Curated and Scheduled for Each Format	Still Professionally Curated and Scheduled for Each Format	Duality of Professionally Curated and Scheduled Alongside User-Generated and Shared	Multiple Creators Produce and Distribute Across Multiple Platforms for Multiple Purposes
Channel	Few Dominant Players With Broad Reach and Tight Control	Proliferation of More Niche Players With Lower Reach and Still Tight Control	Distribution Begins to Shift From Individual Channels Toward Platforms	Platforms Dominate While Individual Channels Disintermediate Among New Players

We've come a long way; yet our travels are far from over. And now, with the chaos in full view, we'll grab our compass known as the Five Global Truths, and we'll travel onward. But let's be clear: everything is now digital. It's time to retire the terms "old media" and "new media." Or, "traditional media" and "digital media." Everything is now digital. And this digital media world in all its complexity is waiting for us to explore.

3

The Five Global Truths

As we journeyed out of the Newtonian Media World and through the turbulent transition toward a digital media era, we quickly realized something: the rules we once trusted were bending in strange and unexpected ways. What had seemed fixed and stable began to blur, stretch, and sometimes even contradict itself. Certainty was gone. Familiar patterns fractured. Predictable systems gave way to chaos.

We weren't just watching history unfold. We were living it. How could we make sense of what we were seeing? When the landscape is stable, a map is enough. But when the terrain itself is shifting—when landmarks disappear and the roads themselves move—you need something else. You need a compass.

A compass doesn't promise a specific destination. It doesn't offer guarantees. It provides a sense of direction. It helps you navigate when the world around you refuses to stay still.

That's exactly why we built the Five Global Truths (Franks 2011). They emerged from close observation of how channels evolved, how content adapted, and how consumers changed. These principles explained the forces that shattered the Newtonian media system and helped us move forward with a bit of clarity in a time of disruption.

The Five Global Truths were never about restoring order. They were about learning to move forward, intelligently and intentionally, through disruption.

In this chapter, we revisit each truth: how it emerged, the technology that catalyzed it, the pioneers who illuminated its power, and its impact on the 3Cs of media—Consumers, Content, and Channels. We also examine how each truth held up over time and how they continue to explain the media realities we face today.

The Five Global Truths Defined

Before we dive deeper, here's a quick orientation to each of the five points on the compass known as The Five Global Truths:

Global Truth #1: Convergence

> Communication channels were once separate and distinct. Each operated through different underlying technologies. But as digital capabilities advanced, those technical differences began to collapse. Channels that had operated independently became increasingly similar in both function and form. An industry built around individual communication systems had to prepare for the convergence of all content onto digital channels. And guess what? They all came with screens.

Global Truth #2: Symbiosis

> Thanks to convergence, the same content (as long as it's digitized) can now appear across many different digital channels. At first, it seemed like channels would now directly compete for audience attention. But a new opportunity emerged: channels could work together by telling different parts of a larger transmedia story. When each channel offers something new and meaningful to the audience, the content experience becomes richer and more rewarding. This is the essence of Symbiosis.

Global Truth #3: Circuits

In the analog era, content moved through fixed pathways—flowing from sender to receiver with little opportunity for sharing or amplification. Digitization changed everything. Media circuits opened, and content could now move freely from one digital channel to another. Content mobility became frictionless. Audiences, once passive receivers, became active accelerators. They could now spread content across vast networks at the speed of share.

Global Truth #4: Brands

Media were once defined by their distribution technology, with each format tied to a specific channel and mode of delivery. But digital convergence broke those ties. As content began to flow across platforms, function alone was no longer enough. To survive—and to thrive—media had to stand for more than the technical capabilities of a channel. They had to become transmedia brands that were built on promises delivered to the audience across any and every channel—today, tomorrow, and into the future.

Global Truth #5: Economics

In the media economy, nothing sustainable is given away for free. Healthy media economics depends on reciprocal value creation across Content, Consumers, and Channels. The relative importance of each of these three components will shift over time. But all must be considered when assessing the health and vitality of the media ecosystem. When any part is neglected or undervalued, the entire system is put at risk.

The Five Global Truths
A Compass to Navigate Digital Media Transformation

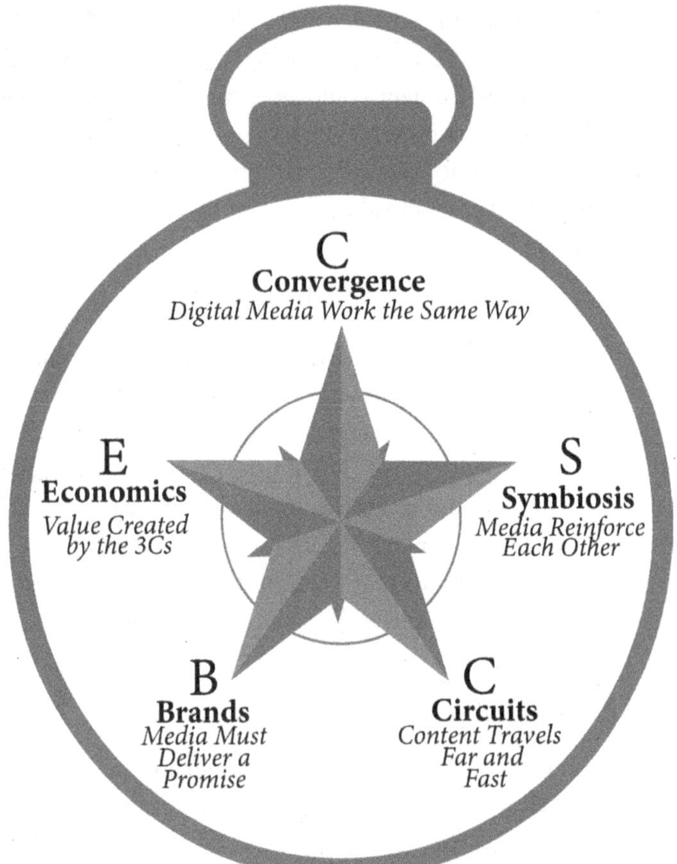

The Story behind Each Global Truth

Now that we've laid out the Five Global Truths, it's time to unpack each one. There's a lot beneath the surface—technological shifts, pioneering responses, and lasting impacts on Consumers, Content, and Channels. Each truth tells its own story, and together, they help us understand how the media ecosystem continues to evolve.

So let's get started.

Global Truth #1: Convergence

Convergence (n.): the merging of distinct technologies, industries or devices into a unified whole. (Source: Merriam-Webster.com)

Back in the Newtonian Media World, the media were separate and distinct. We built an entire industry, along with business models that treated each medium as its own entity. And rightfully so. To readers who don't distinguish much between their television, their laptop, their tablet, or their mobile phone, it may seem unfathomable that we used to rely upon different communication technologies to do different things. The fact that we can talk, we can read, we can watch, we can listen, and we can post all from the same device is a relatively new phenomenon (*c.* 2007)—thank you, iPhone! Digital technology was once confined to computers. But once every media form imaginable began to adopt digital technology, the differences among the media vanished. Welcome to Convergence.

With digital technology came the great screen democracy. Screens used to be limited to televisions and computers. Suddenly, communication modalities that never involved a screen were being delivered on screen devices. Printed words, pictures, music, and our conversations became the domain of screens. As long as content was digitized, it could land on a screen. And the pioneers who caught on took advantage.

Speaking of pioneers, we have to give Apple the credit it is due. This brand, single-handedly, understood the power and attraction of a brilliantly designed digital screen and gave us product innovation that changed the face of every device imaginable. Apple made us rethink what screen devices could be used for. It introduced the idea that a personal computer could be used for more than left-brained pursuits. With the suite of creative tools that was standard on every Mac, we could use our computers to fuel the right sides of our brains as well.

With the launch of the iPhone, Apple transformed mobile phones from talking and messaging devices into *the internet in our pockets* (Jobs 2007). And although Microsoft launched the first tablet computer nearly a decade before, Apple realized that the tablet was more than a smaller, less functional computer. They reimagined the device to blend the screen worlds of work and play. Quite simply, we would not have experienced convergence without Apple's foresight to shift our mindsets toward screen devices. They made us ready and willing to pick up any device available to fulfill any host of wants and needs.

While rethinking screens was an important first step in understanding the forces of convergence, something else quite profound had to happen: the content that we consumed on one device needed to become seamlessly available across all our devices. Apple had the brilliant foresight to make this happen as well. Since Apple used the same basic operating system for all of its devices, consumers could simply pick up the nearest Apple device they had available and consume the same content wherever, whenever, and however they chose. Once the same content could be consumed on any digital device, we were able to tear down the silos that used to confine content to a specific channel. Today, the idea of screen neutrality has become second nature. By tearing down the silos across their own screen devices, Apple shaped an entirely new media experience: one that replaces certainty of a bygone media era with convergence.

While Apple was busy synchronizing digital screens, legacy media companies that were historically confined to specific modes of distribution began to break out of their silos. They began to distribute content in digital formats that could be consumed on and across all these screen devices. To today's reader, this may seem like such an obvious thing to do. But stop and think about the legacy of most media channels: their distribution used to define them. Literally! Newspapers had the word "paper" ingrained in their identities. In television, we used to distinguish between "broadcast" and "cable" networks simply because some networks were around when signals were broadcast over the air while others were formed in the era of cable distribution. And the term "website" quite literally referred to a specific "site" on the World Wide Web. When your industry is named after your legacy, it's no small feat to venture beyond the boundaries of your original channel. However, in the late aughts, nearly every sector within the media ecosystem did just that.

Take Hulu, for example. When it launched in 2008, it was a rare collaboration between broadcast rivals NBC, FOX, and later ABC—an alliance formed to defend against rising digital disruptors. At the time, television was still viewed by many as a passive, even potentially harmful medium—"a vast wasteland," as FCC Chairman Newton Minow (1961) famously called it. Computers, by contrast, were considered tools of enrichment. Hulu's now-famous Super Bowl ad, featuring Alec Baldwin, flipped that script with a smirk: "What are you going to do? Turn off both your TV and your computer?" (Hulu 2009). It was more than a punchline—it marked the moment when screens converged and the lines between media types began to blur. In retrospect, Hulu was a bold experiment in shared control—but once streaming matured, the alliance dissolved. Today, Hulu is solely owned by Disney; the other networks have since launched streaming platforms of their own.

Some legacy media made the transition more gracefully than others. Some are still trying to figure it out. For years, both systems—legacy and digital—existed side by side. Newspapers launched digital editions but continued delivering the morning paper. Television networks built streaming apps while maintaining linear broadcast prime-time lineups. Radio stations still broadcast over the airwaves while streaming content through digital apps. These weren't just transitional experiments—they were signs of a bridge period in which media companies kept one foot in the past while building for the digital future. For some, this coexistence stretched on for decades. The lines didn't blur overnight—they eroded slowly.

One thing, however, became clear: media companies that refused to embrace convergence and clung too tightly to their analog past faced serious consequences. Nowhere is this more evident than in the newspaper industry. National and regional players that adapted early to digital delivery models found ways to survive, even thrive. But those who stayed rooted in print for too long—particularly local newspapers—have struggled or disappeared altogether. According to the Medill Local News Initiative (2023), "More than 2,500 newspapers have closed since 2005. The country continues to lose newspapers at a rate of two per week."

Convergence isn't simply an analog-to-digital force. The forces of convergence reshaped the face of early digital media as well. With the exception of YouTube, most digital media experiences were limited to mainly text and some visuals. To illustrate this point, take a journey through the Facebook archives and you will see the transition for yourself. Facebook was simply evolving in reverse: it was converging to look more like older, more "traditional" media. Even YouTube looks much different today because of convergence. YouTube has evolved from a user-generated video content portal into its own destination for high-quality television programming that carries both libraries of television shows as well as live "event" fares. Even the Super Bowl can now be watched on YouTube!

We've come a long way. Today, those pioneering digital media brands can offer the same rich content experiences that used to be available only on televisions, radios, or in the printed pages of newspapers and magazines. The best content experience wins. It doesn't matter whether a media brand started as an "analog" brand or a "digital" brand. They all compete in the same space, and they all offer similar content experiences.

The force of convergence reshaped all three pillars of the media ecosystem—Consumers, Content, and Channels—in distinct but deeply interconnected ways. For consumers, convergence is now an expectation: they no longer care which screen they're using, only that the content works seamlessly, anytime, anywhere. If it doesn't, they'll move on. For content creators, convergence brought expanded reach but also higher stakes—content can no longer rely on the insulation of the channel or the convenience of limited choice. Attention must be earned. And for channels, convergence was existential. Channels now compete in a landscape where any form of insulation based upon function and form has collapsed.

Faced with an existential crisis, many channels responded by evolving into something more powerful: ecosystems. These weren't just pipelines for distributing content—they became integrated environments that combined content, data, personalization, and commerce into seamless, user-centered experiences. We've entered an era of Super Convergence, where platforms no longer serve a single function. You can watch, read, listen, shop, and chat all in one place. YouTube is now a music service and a video platform. Instagram blends messaging, media, and shopping. Amazon is a storefront, a video library, and a podcast host. The idea that "a screen is a screen is a screen" isn't theoretical—it's reality. But convergence no longer guarantees openness. In fact, new walls are going up. Platforms are reasserting control—locking content inside walled gardens, limiting interoperability, and making it harder to share across ecosystems. It's a defensive maneuver designed to protect economic value. We'll explore these rising walls in later chapters. For now, it's enough to recognize that while convergence remains a defining force, it's no longer frictionless.

Still, as a Global Truth, Convergence endures. It changed the physics of media—dissolving form, demanding quality, and empowering users to access content on their terms. That's not just a trend. That's a foundational shift.

Global Truth #2: Symbiosis

Symbiosis (n.): the living together in more or less intimate association or close union of two dissimilar organisms; a cooperative relationship. (Source: Merriam-Webster.com)

The force of Symbiosis has always been a part of media history. There is little evidence that one communication technology has ever completely destroyed another. Sure, individual media brands have come and gone, but audiences tend to mix the old with the new. According to Marshall McLuhan, when a new communication technology comes along, the old one may become obsolete, but it often finds a new role (McLuhan and McLuhan 1988). It all seems to fit.

Back in the Newtonian Media World, we didn't talk much about media working in symbiosis, even though the potential was always there. The prevailing logic was based on selection. The dominant media channel established the primary connection with the audience, while secondary channels were used to reach others. Because each channel had unique technologies and content formats, content was adapted to fit those forms. Stories might appear in multiple formats, but the same message was simply repackaged—not expanded—and there was little expectation that the same audience would engage with the story across multiple channels.

Toward the end of the Newtonian Era, a different form of storytelling emerged. Content creators began experimenting with transmedia storytelling—a format defined by Professor Henry Jenkins (2006) as narratives that unfold across multiple media platforms, with each channel contributing something new based on what it does best. Audiences were rewarded for traversing channels to experience a richer, more immersive story.

In his book *Convergence Culture*, Jenkins (2006) celebrates *The Matrix* as the first modern transmedia franchise. What began on the fringes of filmmaking and gaming quickly caught on across media. Shows like *Lost, Survivor, American Idol,* and *Heroes* adopted the approach. Journalists also took note—*The Guardian* created an award-winning campaign around "The Three Little Pigs" as a transmedia journalism experiment (*The Guardian* 2012). Savvy marketers caught on. P&G's *Old Spice: The Man Your Man Could Smell Like* was an early example of cross-platform storytelling designed to deepen audience engagement (Old Spice 2010).

As we moved through chaos, something extraordinary happened. The power to shape and expand media narratives shifted beyond traditional storytellers. Digital platforms gave rise to a new class of contributors—the creators. These weren't media professionals; they were everyday people and fans who built upon existing stories and extended narrative worlds in ways legacy gatekeepers never imagined. Jenkins (2006) described this shift as a shared act of storytelling, where world-building becomes a collaboration between content creators and audiences. In some cases, the most talented creators didn't just contribute to stories—they built entire ecosystems around themselves. These creators became media properties in their own right, helping to spark the rise of the creator economy (a topic we'll explore later in the book).

In the early days, transmedia storytelling was cumbersome. Audiences had to traverse entirely different platforms to piece together the full experience. Still, passionate fans embraced the challenge. These pioneering efforts were critical during the analog–digital transition. They allowed creators to experiment with digital formats while staying true to analog roots—and they helped bridge generational divides across media usage.

To support transmedia storytelling at scale, audiences needed a way to navigate. Enter the hashtag. What began as a grassroots Twitter tool soon became an organizing principle across platforms. Hashtags made stories searchable, shareable, and travelable. They offered continuity across fragmented experiences. Over time, recommendation engines and AI tools took over this function, helping audiences discover related content even without knowing what to look for. But it all began with the humble hashtag.

If you want to see how far we've come, just look at *Barbie*. In 2023, Warner Bros. and Mattel launched a film that became much more than a movie—it was a full-blown transmedia ecosystem. The story extended into fashion collaborations, music releases, immersive experiences, social commentary, and endless brand partnerships (Rubin 2023). But what made it truly symbiotic was the role of the audience. Fans became cocreators—remixing the soundtrack, stitching TikToks, building memes, and extending the narrative far beyond the original film. *Barbie* didn't just live on screen. It lived in closets, playlists, timelines, and feeds.

Symbiosis—the second Global Truth—is both an opportunity and a choice made by storytellers. And as we traveled through chaos, we noticed that some media companies expanded their storytelling to take advantage of all the digital formats available to them. Others chose to maintain the singularity of their content, even as the channels around them evolved.

Can both forces coexist? Absolutely. We see it every day. A podcaster may create audio-only content but still use YouTube, Instagram, or TikTok to share snippets and build awareness. That same podcast might be featured in a magazine, on TV, or on social media. The narrative remains singular, but the ecosystem around it is deeply symbiotic. Even when not intentionally designed, transmedia storytelling often happens organically.

Symbiosis continues to reshape the 3Cs of the media ecosystem. Consumers are no longer passive recipients—they expect to engage, respond, and even co-create. Content is no longer tied to one channel—it travels, expands, and adapts. Channels, in turn, do more than just deliver content—they frame it, add meaning, and invite participation. In today's media world, the most successful media experiences don't just reach audiences—they invite them in. Symbiosis makes that possible.

Global Truth #3: Circuits

Circuit (n.): the route traveled, a two-way communication path between points, the complete path of an electric current, including usually the source of electric energy. (Source: Merriam-Webster.com)

Circuitry is a simple but powerful metaphor to describe how content flows across media channels from sender to receiver and back again. During the Newtonian Media Era, media circuits (the pathways by which content flowed from sender to receiver) worked like closed systems. Content flowed in a linear fashion from Point A to Point B with limited disruption. And each analog medium operated on its own circuit. Television content flowed across television circuits (known as broadcast channels), magazine content traveled along magazine circuits (single copy and subscription circulation), and so on. These circuits ran in parallel. There wasn't much mingling.

Who was responsible for turning circuits on or off? Content distribution and flow used to be in the hands of professionals in the media, journalism, and marketing industries. These gatekeepers comprised what was referred to as the formal cultural production system. The audience was the end point in the process—the Point B. And back when most media attracted "mass" audiences, the number on the receiving end was usually substantial.

We developed measurement protocols for each media circuit to determine the size and characteristics of the audience at any given time. This served as a proxy for "who" and "how many" people were exposed to a particular piece of content.

Back then, sharing was cumbersome. If you found a great recipe in a magazine, you might cut it out with scissors, photocopy it, and mail or hand it to someone else. Word of mouth worked in person, but it didn't scale. Audiences may have always had the urge to share, but they lacked the frictionless circuits that would make it easy.

Digital technology changed the circuitry of media. Suddenly, the circuits were open. Content didn't stay put. It started on one channel and seamlessly jumped onto another. Media thought-leader Rishad Tobaccowala referred to this phenomenon as "leaky" media. Others called it displacement. Regardless of the label, the result was the same: it became nearly impossible to contain great content. Once digitized, content became fluid—able to be lifted off one channel and placed onto another with minimal effort.

Social media didn't create open circuits—but it did supercharge them. In the Newtonian era, even if you could lift content, you couldn't easily place it back into the media stream. Social platforms changed that. They gave audiences a place to post and, more importantly, networks through which content could accelerate. Suddenly, anyone could share something across hundreds—or even millions—of followers. Consumers could amplify content at the speed of share.

How prolific was this channel-leaping? Just ask one famous woman: Mona Lisa. If someone asked you to name the media channel that delivers the *Mona Lisa* to the world, you'd probably answer, "the Louvre." But that's only part of the story. If you visited the Louvre today, you'd see hundreds of visitors in front of the iconic painting with their phones held high. One tap—and the *Mona Lisa* has entered a new media circuit, landing on Instagram, Snapchat, or TikTok. She may live in a museum, but she travels across digital networks by the millions.

During our travels through chaos, it was tempting to think of content circuits as one-way streets. A video, meme, or article lifts off one channel and speeds along a social platform into new spaces. But the reverse is also true. Just look at *The Daily Show*'s "Trump Twitter Library." President Trump's tweets—originally posted on social media—were lifted off Twitter and recirculated across television, newspapers, comedy monologues, and even physical installations in New York City (Lang 2017). In an open circuit system, content flows in all directions: from mainstream media to social platforms and back again, creating feedback loops that cross formats, channels, and cultural spaces.

While digital technology opened the circuits, technology was only an accomplice to a much bigger phenomenon. The role of the audience suddenly shifted from recipient to accelerant. What do we mean by acceleration? Think about it. Audiences can act in real time, influencing hundreds, thousands, or even millions of people in their social networks. Word of mouth has existed for centuries. But with open circuits, audiences who are compelled to share what they experience can amplify the reach of any piece of content based on the size of their friends, followers, and email distribution lists. And those secondary audiences can do the same. It goes on and on—exponentially. Consumers have become the most potent media channel in the ecosystem. Frankly, they always were. But their ability to share in the Newtonian Era was far more limited. Today, armed with everyday technology, they accelerate great content to vast networks at the speed of share.

This new open circuitry wasn't all beneficial. It introduced a new set of problems. When content leaked off the originating channel, it became harder for the media company who invested in its creation to make money from it. Copyright lawsuits emerged. Companies attempted to reassert control over where and how far certain content could go.

Today's open circuits continue to reshape the 3Cs of media. Consumers have moved from being passive receivers to becoming powerful accelerants. Content is no longer designed just to be consumed—it's built to be shared, remixed, and reposted. And channels function less as end points and more as amplifiers that enable, shape, and monetize circulation. But while the spirit of open circuitry remains, there are growing constraints. Media companies are reasserting control through paywalls, platform restrictions, and monetization schemes. Circuits are still open—but only to the extent that they can generate revenue. The rise of Walled Gardens is an important theme we'll revisit in the chapters ahead.

Finally, open circuits were a great democratizing agent. You could launch great content in practically any medium. If it was truly worth sharing, it traveled at incredible speeds among well-established networks of hearts and minds. But open circuits also taught us an important lesson: content won't land anywhere—let alone everywhere—if it isn't worth sharing in the first place. This created a renewed focus on the content product itself. Spoken from a true media professional: "Content was, is, and will remain king!"

Global Truth #4: Brands

Brand (n.): a class of goods identified by name as the product of a single firm or manufacturer. (Source: Merriam-Webster.com)

To understand why branding became one of the Five Global Truths guiding us through chaos, you need to know why brands are important in the first place. Brands differentiate products that are otherwise nearly identical in form and function and transform them into something special. They build trust and loyalty in a world oversaturated with choices by providing promises that fuel emotional connections with consumers. While brands still need to meet the functional needs of their product category, powerful brands compete on more than function. A powerful media brand should be able to rise above the chaos of transitioning media channels. It's easier said than done!

Back in the Newtonian Media Era, media companies had an easier time building their businesses off the functional characteristics of their distribution channels. Media distribution pathways were relatively fixed and more proprietary. The technology was not particularly friendly to redundancy. There was only so much room on the broadcast spectrum. There were only so many poles and lines that could run down a street. And a print distribution network was costly and complicated to build.

As we left the Newtonian Media Era and as digital technology became available to any and all media, the functional characteristics of media began to blur together. The forces of convergence meant that distribution pathways were no longer proprietary. Once media content was digitized, it lost the safety of distribution silos suited for specific formats: broadcast, newsprint, glossy paper, cable conduit, and so on. Even what was once proprietary to a computer screen or mobile device faced the same competition from a host of legacy media that migrated into the digital media space. All digital content travels along the same digital highway. Any media enterprise that defined its strategy solely by its means of distribution ran into trouble. Suddenly, competition for the time and attention of audiences was coming from just about anywhere and everywhere.

Digital distribution further complicated matters, proving inexpensive and accessible to anyone. With $10–$20 to register a domain name and basic software like WordPress or Squarespace, anyone could enter the media business. We transitioned from a landscape of scarcity to one of abundance. There was more media than we knew what to do with!

Unfortunately, transmedia brands that could break through the confines of their distribution channels were few and far between. All too often, brands built their identities from their mode of distribution. The rise and fall of MTV is a prime example. In August 1981, MTV signed on with its famous "Video Killed the Radio Star" music video, revolutionizing the idea of music delivered on television. MTV became the media brand of an entire generation. Those of us who witnessed this phenomenon firsthand were labeled "The MTV Generation." Over time, music migrated from television screens to digital screens. But MTV didn't follow suit. It clung to its identity as a cable television network, ceding the digital music space to the likes of Sony, Apple, and others. Today, MTV is a mere shadow of its former self.

The MTV story isn't unique. Consider CNN. It's hard to establish an identity beyond cable news when your name, "Cable News Network," ties you to the channel. HBO started the same way—as Home Box Office.

But there were glimmers of hope. Take ESPN. When ESPN first entered the picture in 1979, the idea of a cable network fully dedicated to sports was provocative. But ESPN understood that cable distribution was not the story. At the time, sports coverage was accessible on various channels: television, radio, newspapers, and the like. But ESPN was different. It built a brand on the idea that it would not simply distribute sports content over a cable conduit; rather, it would serve sports fans.

ESPN's mission, "To serve sports fans wherever sports are watched, listened to, discussed, debated, read about, or played," shapes everything it does. This commitment infuses a unique personality into ESPN's content, enabling it to meet sports fans where they are. As long as ESPN delivers its promise to sports fans, the brand can transcend any channel.

Has ESPN faced challenges from its primary distribution channel? Absolutely. It grapples with the financial strain of competing in a new digital landscape shaped by convergence. Yet, a weaker brand would have collapsed. ESPN continues to navigate emerging channels serving sports fans. While its financials may not be perfect, the opportunity remains.

Ironically, even as new digital media companies came onto the scene, many of them made the same mistake. Take Netflix, for instance. Its name implies movie access over the internet, tying the company to a specific distribution mode. The branding worked well for a time, but as Netflix evolved into a producer, distributor, and cultural force, it outgrew its own label. Even the most innovative players can fall into old patterns.

So what we have here isn't an explanatory truth as much as a cautionary one. Convergence will take away the distinction between channels. Branding is necessary to survive. We've seen this in many other industries where brands saved products from becoming commodities. It's time for media to catch on—or fall victim to sameness.

That said, we're seeing some shiny examples: one old, and one new. The New York Times has become a destination brand for trusted, in-depth reporting, multimedia storytelling, and even lifestyle products. Others, like NPR (National Public Radio) or National Geographic, quietly evolved into multi-format experiences without abandoning their editorial DNA. These brands succeeded not because of their technology—but because of their clarity of purpose.

And then there's Google. Despite the real threats it faces—from antitrust litigation to increased regulatory scrutiny—Google has built something few other tech companies have: an enduring place in the hearts and minds of its users. Google doesn't just functionally provide information access; rather, the brand is built on the promise of "organizing the world's information and making it universally accessible and useful" (Google n.d.). That brand promise transcends product features, screen formats, and even business models.

Why does it matter for us to get this right? Let's consider the 3Cs. In today's ecosystem of content overload and digital clutter, the brand isn't just a logo—it's a trustmark. In a search-driven environment, where the same news story might appear across dozens of indistinguishable sites, consumers instinctively gravitate toward the brand they trust most. That's more important than ever in an era when content itself can become commoditized. Branding isn't fluff. It's navigation. And only a transmedia brand—one that delivers on its promise across any channel, regardless of form or function—will be able to follow the future trajectory of evolving media. The rest will be left behind, their relevance fading as fast as the channels they were built upon. For content creators, a strong brand gives shape and direction to the stories they produce. And for channels, branding becomes a way to frame experience beyond functionality. As the distinctions between delivery systems dissolve, brand becomes the anchor.

Currently, the media ecosystem would barely earn a passing grade. As we traveled through chaos, we found a landscape littered with technology companies that didn't move beyond their functional product offerings toward something more permanent and meaningful in their customers' lives. Remember Myspace? Vine videos? AOL, anyone? The list goes on. All those once shiny objects are now nothing more than discarded litter alongside the vast superhighway. It's time we got this fundamental truth right.

Global Truth #5: Economics

Economics (n.): a social science concerned chiefly with description and analysis of the production, distribution, and consumption of goods and services. (Source: Merriam-Webster.com)

In the end, it all comes down to money. The media business is primarily a for-profit enterprise—and nothing is sustainable if given away for free. As technology consultant Shelly Palmer (2022) succinctly put it: "I pay, you pay, or someone else pays." While his phrasing was simple, it reflects a much larger truth about media economics: value must come from each of the three Cs—Content, Consumers, and Channels. Some content is valuable enough that consumers will pay directly for it, like a movie rental or a digital download. Other content, such as the user-generated stories that populate your social feed, may not be something consumers will pay for—but advertisers will, in order to reach those audiences. And channels themselves can generate revenue by offering subscriptions that unlock access to a full library of content. In practice, most media models blend these revenue sources into a web of value creation.

During the Newtonian Media Era, economic models were relatively stable. Broadcast television and radio were free to the audience and advertiser-supported. Print media charged both subscribers and advertisers. Cable bundled dozens of channels into a single fee, with some premium networks operating ad free. The business models were distinct, consistent, and predictable.

Then came digital. In the early days of the internet, the economic model resembled broadcast: content was free to audiences and supported (or at least supplemented) by advertising. But unlike broadcast, advertisers were slow to follow. Media companies gave away digital ads as "added value" for legacy buys or adopted direct-response pricing models like cost per click (CPC). This undervalued system generated only a fraction of legacy revenue, leading media executive Jeff Zucker (2008) to lament, "We traded analog dollars for digital pennies."

This might help explain why professional content producers were slow to move their content off analog channels and onto digital platforms. If you were making money from traditional advertising revenue, you couldn't afford to accept digital pennies. And since the audience wasn't paying, you couldn't make up the difference. It was a lose-lose proposition.

So what happened instead? We had all this excess digital channel capacity without enough high-quality content to fill it. Enter the Creator. These new digital-native producers posted user-generated content directly onto digital platforms, often earning money through revenue-sharing models tied to digital ads. Creators had less overhead and could survive on smaller margins. The economics worked—at least for a while.

But the dominant model in the early days of digital—direct-response advertising—had a dark side. It incentivized quantity over quality, giving rise to clickbait and MFA (made for advertising) sites. These farms flooded the internet with exaggerated or misleading content, prioritizing clicks over truth and degrading public trust. The content itself became a casualty of the economic model that prioritized immediate interaction over meaningful engagement.

Eventually, pioneers stepped in to challenge the status quo. Netflix and The New York Times rejected the assumption that digital content must be free and solely ad-supported. Netflix launched its streaming platform in 2007 with an ad-free subscription model that proved audiences would pay for quality. It took fifteen years, but eventually Netflix introduced an ad-supported tier in 2022. Consumers now have a choice: pay a lower subscription fee and watch with ads, or pay more for an ad-free experience. The time was right for advertising-supported subscription tier because unlike the early "digital pennies" advertising days, Netflix could now command high CPMs (cost per 1,000 audience impressions served)—comparable to those of television—reflecting the value advertisers place on Netflix's high-quality, brand-safe content.

The New York Times introduced its paywall back in 2011, creating a sustainable revenue stream from readers without abandoning advertisers altogether. This hybrid model preserved traditional strengths while adapting to a digital world. Over time, The Times expanded beyond journalism into cooking, games, wellness, and audio—diversifying its value and proving that media companies could both broaden and deepen their relationships with consumers in the digital terrain and become profitable while at it.

While these two pioneers demonstrated the new economic potential of digital media, not all is well across the board. Today, we're seeing growing tension among competing economic models. Subscription fatigue is real, as consumers grow overwhelmed by the number of services vying for a slice of their wallet. At the same time, ad-supported models face the challenge of increasing clutter and waning attention. Many consumers are rethinking how much content they truly need—and how much they're willing to pay. They churn in and out of services, bundle content with other purchases, or opt for lower-cost, ad-supported options. In response, media companies are forced to experiment with a mix of hybrid access, tiered pricing, and cross-subsidization in search of economic stability. Not all are successful (Malthouse et al. 2024).

The moral of the story? Without a viable economic model, nothing else matters. The media industry can't build for the future if it doesn't know how to fund it. And while the first wave of digital disruption is behind us, the next wave of economic pressure is just beginning. In the chapters ahead, we'll explore how media economics are increasingly influenced by other business models—particularly commerce. These hybrid models are reshaping how content is monetized and valued across platforms, and we'll cover this extensively in the coming chapters of the book.

Regardless of its source, the truth remains: economic vitality is essential to the future of the media industry, solidifying it as one of the Five Global Truths.

Using All Five Global Truths to Explain Modern Media

Each of the truths on their own or in combination with the others explained how the Newtonian Media World broke down and how we've arrived at our current state. While our story isn't over, the part of the story that deals with the transition to a digital media world is complete. And the Five

Global Truths got us here. Albert Einstein is often credited with saying, "If you can't explain it simply, you don't understand it well enough." Here's a simple explanation using the Five Global Truths to explain the digital media world as it exists today:

> Media are no longer confined to a specific channel. Today, any media company can set up shop on any digital channel available. While media companies can choose to focus on a single mode of delivery, it's not a necessity, it's a choice. And those same media companies can now tell transmedia stories to take advantage of how individual media build upon and complement each other. With the right form of storytelling, audiences are rewarded for crossing channels to immerse themselves in a story, and each channel can contribute based on its strengths. If media companies create content worth sharing, the open circuitry of the digital media landscape enables consumers to accelerate that content across vast networks at the speed of share. Moreover, media companies that understand branding can capitalize on these changes, traveling to where consumers want to go and where existing and emerging channels will take them. Those stuck in a particular mode of distribution will likely struggle. No sector of this new media landscape is immune to economic challenges. The economics of the mass media era are behind us, and the new economics require a focus on earning a fair return on all three components of the media equation—Content, Channels, and Consumers.

4

New Players in a New Land

Today's digital media landscape is filled with both possibility and complexity. What was once the domain of professionally run media companies is now populated by a diverse set of players. While all of them qualify as "media" under the definition of 3Cs—each must provide a Channel, offer Content, and attract Consumers—their motivations, business strategies, and audience relationships are far from identical.

In this chapter, we're going to do more than simply name the new players. We're going to explore how they behave as media. And we'll use the 3Cs as a diagnostic guidepost to guide our understanding.

For each player in the modern media landscape, we'll ask:

- Is their channel a singular, brand-defined environment—or part of a shared space that is governed by others?
- What role does content play in their strategy—is it the sole reason for being, or does it support something else?
- And what mindset is the consumer in when they engage—are they here to consume media, to shop, to connect, or for something else entirely?

Let's unpack each of these dimensions before we meet the players themselves.

The distribution channel has always played a powerful role in media. In the Newtonian Media Era, channels were limited, centralized, and often exclusive. A broadcaster did not own their spot on the spectrum; they had to license it from the FCC. But with that license, they were able to air their

How New Players Operate as Media: A 3Cs Diagnostic View

Channel

Is the content delivered in a dedicated environment, or one shared with others?

Singular, Brand-Defined Space ⟵⟶ Shared, Platform-Based Space

Content

Is content the product, or a means to another end?

Content-as-Product ⟵⟶ Content-as-Vehicle

Consumer

What mindset is the audience in when they engage?

Media Consumption Mode ⟵⟶ Non-Media Modes (Social, Shopping, Utility)

programming in a space that was dedicated solely to their brand. In today's digital landscape, that sense of exclusivity varies widely. Some players deliver content through singular, brand-defined environments—spaces like websites, streaming apps, or newsletters where the experience is curated and uninterrupted by competing voices. Others operate within shared platforms such as social feeds, video hubs, or retail marketplaces where their content appears alongside that of competitors, influencers, and countless other contributors. When we talk about each player's channel strategy, we're considering the distinctiveness of the environment. Is it a destination built around a single enterprise, or is it comingled with others in a noisy feed?

Not all content is created for the same purpose. For some, content is the product; it's what gets measured, valued, and monetized. But for others, content is a tool. It's designed to sell something else, drive traffic, enhance loyalty, and serve a broader brand or commercial objective. The key question is whether the content exists for its own sake or as a means to another end.

Audience attention doesn't exist in a vacuum. People show up to media experiences with different goals. Sometimes they're deliberately seeking out content. They want to be informed, entertained, or inspired (Peck and Malthouse 2010). Other times, they're shopping, solving a problem, or catching up with friends. The mindset they bring shapes how they engage, how long they stay, and what kind of value they take away. That's why we consider not just who the audience is, but why they're showing up in the first place.

Each dimension of the 3Cs will help us better understand how today's media players operate. It's worth noting that no media player exists in just one place on this framework. Many operate across a spectrum—sometimes delivering content in controlled environments they define, and sometimes relying on shared spaces governed by others. The diagnostic guideposts of the 3Cs aren't meant to lock anyone into a category. Instead, they give us a flexible way to understand how each player behaves as media and where their strategies are most concentrated.

New Players in a New Land
Digital Transformation Creates Unprecedented Access

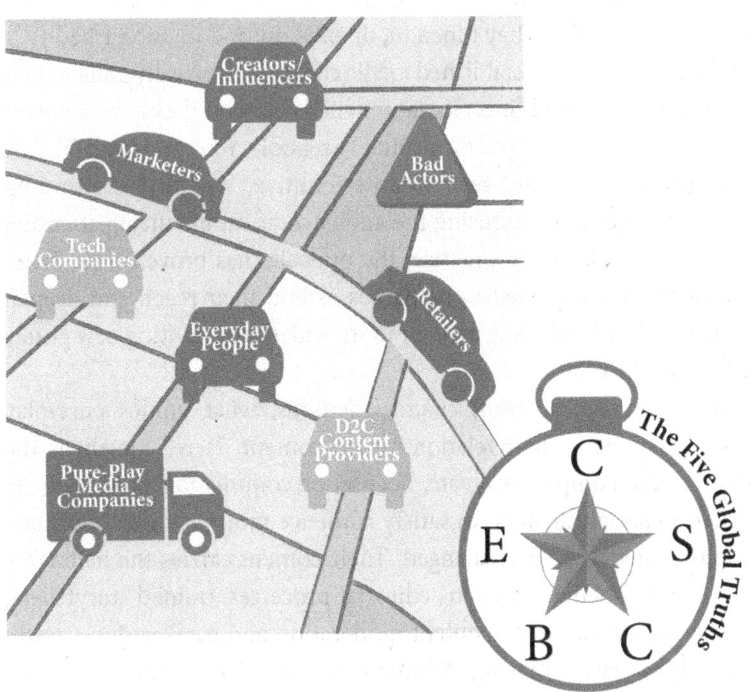

Pure-Play Media Companies

Let's begin with the media companies whose primary business is and always has been media. These are the organizations that live at the heart of the industry. Their product is content. Their customers are audiences. And their revenue depends on their ability to monetize both. Some are long-established players with legacy roots in analog formats. Others are digital natives that launched with the internet. But whether old or new, their core business revolves around the same essential dynamic: creating content that serves audience needs and distributing it across media channels they control—or at least carefully manage.

Historically, pure-play media companies operated on their own media channels. A television network had a fixed position on the dial, and it was solely responsible for the programming that aired on the channel. A newspaper defined its front page. A magazine curated the stories, visuals, and voices that appeared between its covers. And radio disc jockeys—far more than just personalities—served as powerful curators, hand-selecting the music and guiding the mood of the moment. These environments were exclusive and brand-defined. Audiences knew what they were getting when they tuned in, opened up, and/or subscribed.

Today, even the most established media companies have diversified their channel strategies. In addition to their owned channels they also maintain a presence across shared platforms like Facebook, YouTube, and TikTok. At first glance, this might seem counterintuitive. Wouldn't showing up in so many places risk confusing the audience or cannibalizing attention from their home base? In practice, the opposite has proven true. These shared platforms help media companies extend their reach and deepen relationships by distributing content more widely and inviting new points of entry into the brand.

Across all these different channel settings, what unifies pure-play media companies is their relationship to content. Here, content is the product. These companies create, license, or commission professionally produced material intended to satisfy audience motives: to be informed, entertained, inspired, or challenged. Their content carries the hallmarks of professional media—rigorous editorial processes, trained storytellers, and experienced curators. Content moderation and gatekeeping are still very much in play. While algorithmic recommender systems may guide what shows up next in a feed or viewing queue, a human team is still programming the content strategy behind the scenes.

This distinction matters. For the consumer, pure-play media companies offer a trusted environment designed around their expectations. Audiences turn to these players with purpose. They want to stream a high-quality drama, catch up on the day's headlines, or learn from experts. The content is central, the experience is (mostly) curated, and the media brand plays an important role in shaping trust, tone, and value. These companies succeed not by monetizing some other business through media but by serving audiences through media itself.

GQ stands as a clear example of a pure-play media company. Its business is squarely focused on creating professionally produced content and monetizing both the content product and the audience product. Through advertising, sponsorships, branded content, and licensing, GQ turns its editorial and visual authority into revenue streams. It doesn't use content to sell something else—it sells the content itself and the attention that content earns from a style- and culture-conscious audience.

GQ's origins lie in print. As a legacy magazine brand, its original distribution channel was exclusive and brand-defined, delivered monthly into the hands of loyal subscribers and newsstand readers. The magazine curated every page with intention, offering a highly controlled editorial experience shaped by professional editors, stylists, and contributors. That print foundation still anchors the brand today, but the media landscape has evolved, and GQ has evolved with it.

Its website now serves as the brand's primary editorial hub, extending the print identity into a digital environment that allows for daily publishing, interactivity, and real-time relevance. From there, GQ's content reaches audiences across platforms such as YouTube, Instagram, TikTok, and newsletters. At times, GQ uses Convergence to repurpose content across multiple channels and expand its reach. At other times, it leans into Symbiosis, creating original pieces for specific platforms that complement the core brand experience. These efforts don't fragment the audience—they reinforce the brand's presence and deepen engagement.

Why do audiences show up? GQ serves a specific consumer mindset: readers and viewers come for inspiration, expertise, and cultural relevance. Whether it's fashion advice, grooming recommendations, or interviews with influential figures, GQ delivers content that aligns with the audience's goals. And even as algorithmic tools help distribute and surface that content, the editorial hand remains visible. The brand experience is still programmed—curated intentionally, shaped by professionals, and consistent across every channel where GQ appears.

Direct-to-Consumer (D2C) Content Providers

Some of the most compelling media today doesn't come from traditional media companies at all. It comes from content owners—especially those with high-demand, high-value programming—who historically relied on media companies to reach their audiences. In the analog era, content owners didn't have much choice. Channel capacity was scarce. If you wanted to follow your favorite sports team, hear from a trusted journalist, or experience the next chapter of your favorite story IP from a brand like Marvel or Lucasfilm, you had to rely on the media companies that controlled the channels. Content owners built their businesses by licensing those rights to the media gatekeepers who controlled access. In many cases, this was a good deal. Rights fees were substantial, and the reach was unmatched.

But distribution constraints began to loosen toward the end of the analog era. With the rise of cable and satellite, channel capacity expanded, and we started to see the early formation of direct-to-consumer (D2C) models. Sports led the way. Teams and leagues began to experiment with their own dedicated channels—regional sports networks that gave them greater control over their content, branding, and revenue streams. The Chicago Cubs offer a compelling example. For decades, the Cubs were broadcast on WGN, a superstation that brought the team into homes across the country. But when the Cubs launched Marquee Sports Network, it wasn't about getting on television; it was about controlling the business model behind it. The team's owners were no longer just licensing games to a broadcaster; they were now operating the channel itself, shaping not just what aired but how it was packaged and monetized.

The shift accelerated in the digital era. With streaming, apps, and subscription platforms, content owners could finally reach fans directly, without needing a cable box or broadcast partner. Consider the case of

Major League Baseball (MLB) and the creation of Major League Baseball Advanced Media (MLBAM). Originally formed to manage the digital rights for Major League Baseball, MLBAM launched MLB.tv, giving fans access to out-of-market games directly through a league-controlled platform. It's a powerful example of a content owner going direct to its audience. And while MLB still licenses a large portion of its content to traditional and digital broadcasters, it also now operates in parallel as a media company itself.

That blend—some content distributed through partners, some offered directly to fans—is the model that defines today's D2C content providers. And what makes it work is fandom. These audiences don't show up casually. They seek out this content because they care. They follow their team. They trust a particular voice. They want access, proximity, and consistency. These are not audiences browsing aimlessly; they're fans who will cross platforms and pay premiums to stay connected.

While many D2C content providers now operate their own apps, subscriptions, or streaming destinations, they don't stop there. Much like pure-play media companies, they also extend their reach by sharing content across public platforms like TikTok, Instagram, YouTube, Facebook, and more. These shared channels help drive awareness, highlight key moments, and reinforce brand loyalty. At times, they repurpose core content for mass distribution. At other times, they share new content that invites audiences deeper into the owned ecosystem. It's not just distribution—it's strategy.

As audiences fragment and distribution pathways proliferate, D2C content providers represent a new kind of media company. They may not have started with channels of their own, but they've built direct relationships with consumers that many traditional media companies envy. And increasingly, they know how to use those relationships to their full advantage.

Marketers Enter the Media Business

For decades, marketers funded the media industry. Their advertising dollars sustained media companies and helped to underwrite access for audiences. But today, many marketers have entered the media realm themselves. You may have heard the term "owned media"—a phrase that refers to any content or platform a brand or organization creates and controls outright. This includes websites, blogs, social media profiles, mobile apps, email newsletters, loyalty portals, and other environments where the brand can communicate without paying a third party for access to the audience.

At first glance, marketer-owned media can resemble the D2C content models we just discussed. But there's an important distinction: marketers don't monetize the content itself or the attention it receives. Instead, they use content as a means to another end—to influence behavior, drive commerce, build loyalty, or shape perception. Owned media allows for direct interaction, audience data collection, and more personalized brand experiences.

On the surface, owned media may appear to be a cost-saving alternative to traditional advertising. There's no media bill, no cost per impression, and no competition for placement. But it's not free. Content creation still carries real costs—in time, budget, and creative energy. Many organizations underestimate what it takes to build an audience and hold attention. If you want to play in the media space, you have to act like a media company. That means putting the audience's unmet wants, needs, and expectations front and center. They're not showing up for a product pitch—they're showing up for content that speaks to their interests, emotions, or goals. Just like any other media channel, you have to earn their time by delivering something that informs, entertains, supports, or inspires.

Marketers distribute content across both owned environments (like websites and mobile apps) and shared platforms (like social channels and video networks). Owned channels offer control and access to first-party data. Shared platforms offer scale and discoverability—but with trade-offs in context, placement, and competition. Smart marketers understand how to balance these priorities by tailoring content and distribution to the mindset of the consumer and the strength of the relationship.

LEGO understands the power of content to fuel imagination and deepen emotional connection. LEGO puts as much care into its owned media experience as it does into its product line. Just visit the LEGO YouTube channel—home to story-driven animation, play-centered tutorials, and inspiring builds. With more than 19 million subscribers at the time of this writing, LEGO has become a standout among brands using content to elevate engagement. The brand may not call itself a media company—but it acts like one.

You can get an audience to show up on your owned media if they have a reason to—whether they're searching for answers, exploring solutions, or checking out a brand they've heard about. But getting them to come back? That requires thinking like a media company. Your content has to be curated with intention, delivering a sense of flow and value that aligns with why audiences turn to media in the first place. Easier said than done. It's expensive. It requires editorial skill and professional storytellers. But many marketers already hold the subject-matter expertise needed to go head-to-head with the best media brands. If they invest in content development—and if they recognize it must be media first, commerce later—they can become formidable players in the media space.

Retailers Bridge the Gap between Content and Commerce

One of the key benefits marketers realized by launching their owned media channels was the direct relationship they could establish with their customers. It didn't take long for retailers to recognize the value of that same direct connection. Historically, retailers served as intermediaries—connecting consumers with brands that didn't sell directly to the public. But as digital platforms matured and first-party data became more valuable, retailers saw a bigger opportunity: to transform their own proprietary channels into media businesses.

Retailers sit on one of the most powerful owned channel assets in the media ecosystem. Their websites, mobile apps, loyalty programs, and even in-store screens are transaction-enabled environments—places where attention, intent, and action converge. These proprietary channels aren't just conduits for messaging—they are engines of commerce, infused with rich first-party data collected from real, recurring customer interactions. This allows retailers to offer high-performance advertising opportunities, delivering precisely targeted messages just moments before a potential sale.

This is the foundation of the retail media network (RMN): a digital advertising platform operated by a retailer that allows brands to promote their products directly within the retailer's owned properties. Brands can place ads across the retailer's site, app, or in-store screens—reaching consumers at the point of decision. With the retailer's data powering the targeting, these placements are not just contextual—they're precise. And with commerce just a click away, they offer a form of marketing that's both measurable and actionable.

But let's be clear: the consumer's motive in these environments is not media consumption—it's shopping. That changes everything. Audiences aren't here to be entertained or informed in the traditional sense. They're looking for value, inspiration, convenience, or confirmation. If retailers want to operate as media companies, they must deliver content that enhances the shopping experience—not one that interrupts it. The channel is there, and the consumer is present at a critical moment. But without meaningful content, it's just shopper marketing in digital form.

That's why a growing debate has emerged in the industry: Are retail media networks truly "media" as we define them using the framework of 3Cs? Or are they simply the modern evolution of traditional shopper marketing? On the surface, it may sound like a semantic issue—but the implications are real. The answer determines where budgets come from (media vs. shopper marketing), who controls spending in RMNs, and how performance is measured. In our view, the answer lies in the third "C": Content. Retailers already have the channel, and they already reach the consumer. But unless they invest in content that earns audience attention and adds value to the journey, they fall short of being true media players.

Some retailers are starting to rise to that challenge. Specialty brands like Sephora and Lululemon have invested in in-house content teams to produce videos, articles, and experiences that align with their brand identity and customer lifestyle. Larger retailers—including Target, Walmart, Amazon, and Aldi—have taken a different route, partnering with venerable magazine publishers and media companies to bring editorial credibility and storytelling skill into their content ecosystems. In both models, the goal is the same: to create content that enhances the shopping experience while deepening engagement.

Walmart Connect is a prime example of a retail media network that's evolving toward a more sophisticated content-and-commerce strategy.

Walmart already owns one of the most visited digital shopping platforms in the world and possesses a vast reservoir of first-party customer data—giving it powerful channel control and consumer access. But in recent years, Walmart has also begun experimenting with content experiences that blend utility and inspiration. Through partnerships with Publishers and Creators, and initiatives like livestream shopping and recipe-driven commerce, Walmart Connect is shaping an environment where media doesn't just support shopping—it becomes part of it. These efforts reflect a recognition that, in order to compete not only for transactions but for attention, content must play an active and intentional role.

When done well, this content isn't just decoration—it's a media asset. It helps brands and retailers earn attention, drive sales, and collect valuable engagement signals. And as the economics of content–commerce continue to evolve, this hybrid approach may create new sources of revenue that go beyond traditional media's reliance on either audiences or advertisers. The result is something we haven't quite seen before: a media company embedded within a marketplace where content earns attention and commerce captures the outcome.

Technology Companies Become Players in the Media Ecosystem

Technology companies didn't start out as media companies. In the early days of the digital era, their role was infrastructure. And while not all tech is becoming "media," two notable pioneers—Google and Apple—expanded beyond their roots to become what we now recognize as players in the media ecosystem. But this transition from technology to media didn't happen overnight.

Google helped organize the web and made it searchable. Apple created the devices and operating systems that brought digital content into our hands. Together, they built the digital pipelines—laying the tracks for others to build destinations in the emerging media terrain.

At first, both companies acted as facilitators. Google connected audiences to content created by others. Apple provided the hardware and marketplace through which that content could be purchased and consumed. In both cases, they enabled distribution and access, not production. And for that facilitation, they earned revenue—through ad sales, platform commissions, and device purchases.

But over time, something shifted. These digital channels became more valuable not only because of the content they connected but because of the scale of consumers they attracted and the rich behavioral data they collected along the way. Still, one piece remained out of reach: content they could call their own. And that's where the next stage of evolution began.

Google entered the digital realm as an aggregator whose role was to help organize the content of others and make it searchable. Their mission was to "organize the world's information and make it universally accessible and useful" (Google n.d.). Yet, they did not remain a neutral third party in their quest. The acquisition of YouTube in 2006 was a transformative move, turning the platform into the world's largest video-sharing service. Through YouTube, Google has expanded its reach, not just as a content aggregator but as a content creator, hosting a blend of user-generated content, original programming via YouTube Originals, and exclusive shows. This strategy has bolstered Google's position in the digital media ecosystem, generating substantial ad revenue and subscription fees.

In 2017, Google further solidified its presence in the media industry with the launch of YouTube TV, a streaming service offering live television, on-demand video, and cloud-based DVR from more than eighty-five television networks, including the major broadcast networks and cable channels. YouTube TV provides an alternative to traditional cable TV, emphasizing the shift toward digital streaming platforms and reflecting Google's commitment to evolving its media offerings.

Beyond video, Google has also made significant inroads into digital news with Google News and Google News Showcase, partnering with publishers worldwide. These initiatives aim to support journalism while enhancing the user experience with curated news content. Additionally, Google's Play Store serves as a vast digital marketplace for movies, TV shows, books, and music, integrating various media formats into its ecosystem and reinforcing its footprint in digital media distribution.

Apple, on the other hand, has seamlessly blended technology with media production. Apple TV+, launched in November 2019, marked its bold entry into the streaming industry, producing acclaimed series like *The Morning Show* and *Ted Lasso*, which have received critical acclaim and awards. This move has positioned Apple as a formidable competitor to established streaming services like Netflix and Amazon Prime Video.

Apple Music, introduced in 2015, has also become a key player in the digital music market, offering exclusive releases and a substantial user base, challenging Spotify and other music streaming giants. Furthermore, Apple's investments in podcasts and acquisitions of prominent podcast production companies underscore its strategy to diversify its media offerings. Through these ventures, Apple has created a robust media ecosystem, seamlessly integrating its hardware and software products with its content services, enhancing the overall user experience.

Both companies have leveraged their extensive distribution ecosystems by adding their own content domains to ultimately create a comprehensive and engaging user experience. In essence, they transformed their dumb pipes and now deliver upon the 3Cs of media themselves to become influential players in the media industry. They always had the channel. In fact, it was their channels that set the stage for everyone else. They had consumer attention, given the scale and stickiness of their platforms. And once they established branded content domains—through creation, curation, or licensing—the 3Cs were complete.

The Creators Find Their Voice

Enter the Creators. You'll recall that as we explored the characteristics of the new digital world, we noted that channel capacity expanded exponentially. There was far more capacity than we could ever fill with existing, professionally produced content. And, remember, in the early days of digital transformation, legacy media companies were slow to migrate their content onto digital channels—and for good reason. The Creators filled that void, and they are now a vital part of the digital media landscape.

In the digital context, the term *Creator* refers to individuals who produce and share original content with a specific audience on platforms such as YouTube, Instagram, TikTok, or personal blogs. Creators encompass a wide range of content producers. They craft various forms of content—from videos and podcasts to written articles, images, and livestreams.

But having content alone wasn't enough. What enabled the Creator Economy to flourish was access to channels. The rise of open platforms gave individuals the ability to publish at scale—no permission required. These platforms, built for public sharing, created a form of democratized distribution that didn't exist in the analog world. Anyone with a voice and a perspective could now reach an audience, and the playing field was dramatically leveled. Channel capacity wasn't just expanded—it was unlocked for all.

Just as the channels opened up, something shifted on the consumer side too. We began to see a breakdown in trust in formal institutions— governments, corporations, and even legacy media. A new media generation was looking for different voices, and when they found them, they were all in. Creators offered something personal, unfiltered, and, by design, interactive. Their influence didn't come from a network logo or a professional pedigree; it came from the audience that chose to follow them.

That trust didn't go unnoticed. Creators have become so integral to the media ecosystem that marketers are recalibrating their media strategies around them. Unilever's Dove brand, for example, has been at the forefront of campaigns that reject overly polished portrayals of beauty in favor of authentic, Creator-led storytelling. The brand has made a deliberate shift in its media mix to align with Creators who reflect its values—recognizing that influence now lives in trusted voices, not traditional ad formats.

Successful Creators are distinguished by their commitment to consistency and strategy. They upload content regularly and follow a deliberate plan to engage their audience, fostering a loyal following. This dedication to audience connection is a hallmark of their success. They often invest in production value by using professional equipment and editing software, and they actively respond to comments, participate in social discussions, and collaborate with their fans. In doing so, they build a sense of community around their personal brands.

Why go to all this trouble? Because a key aspect of the Creator Economy is monetization. Creators often seek to earn revenue through various channels, including ad revenue, sponsorships, merchandise sales, and direct fan support via platforms like Patreon or membership programs. For some, this has become a viable and highly lucrative business model— one that, in the digital realm, can rival (and even exceed) the revenues generated by legacy media.

In 2022, *Forbes* began publishing its "Top Creator" list. In 2023, the fifty honorees on this list "...harnessed a combined 2.6 billion followers to haul in an estimated $700 million in earnings" (Bertoni 2023). Who topped the list? According to *Forbes*, Jimmy Donaldson—better known as MrBeast—led with over 300 million followers across YouTube.

Creators exemplify the 3Cs paradigm of media companies. They rely on public, scalable digital platforms to reach their audiences. The content they produce is often of relatively high quality and consistently tailored to engage and entertain. And they cultivate dedicated consumer bases who don't just passively consume but actively participate in their success. Through this strategic alignment with Channel, Content, and Consumer, Creators have become powerful, community-driven forces in the digital media ecosystem.

Bad Actors Leverage Opportunities to Make Money

We just finished celebrating Creators who used the explosion in channel capacity for good by offering new voices, building loyal communities, and reshaping what media could be. But not everyone used that same excess capacity with such integrity. Unfortunately, as Marshall McLuhan once observed, every new technology, when pushed to its extreme, reverses into the opposite of its original intention (McLuhan and McLuhan 1988). Alongside the rise of the Creator Economy came a darker force: the bad actors—those who saw opportunity, not to inform or inspire, but to exploit.

All that excess digital media supply was waiting to be gamed. Clickbait farms and made-for-advertising (MFA) websites began pumping out vast volumes of content designed to manipulate algorithms rather than serve audiences. These operations optimize for revenue, not relevance. They produce headlines designed to provoke curiosity or outrage, then monetize the attention that follows—regardless of whether the content delivers any real value.

Clickbait means exactly what it says: we're being baited to click. The psychological pull is powerful. It's driven by urgency, novelty, or emotional triggers. And this is where the audience plays a role. We're not passive victims. Our behavior—our clicks, likes, and shares—is the fuel that drives the engine. The success of bad actors depends on our response to the bait.

Clickbait farms have become big business. You may have clicked on content served up by companies like Taboola or Outbrain. If so, you're certainly not alone. According to AdExchanger, Taboola earned $1.4 billion in calendar year 2022, while Outbrain brought in more than $1 billion (Schreurs 2023). The scale is staggering. The Association of National Advertisers (ANA), in its 2023 *Programmatic Media Supply Chain Transparency Study*, found that MFA websites accounted for 21 percent of impressions and 15 percent of spend in the open programmatic marketplace (Association of National Advertisers 2023).

But the stakes have grown beyond wasted clicks and empty headlines. Today, the clickbait ecosystem also traffic in misinformation and disinformation. What began as a strategy for maximizing ad revenue now fuels ideological agendas. Misleading headlines and manipulative narratives spread rapidly through social media, designed to polarize, confuse, or reinforce filter bubbles. According to a 2022 Pew Research Center study, 64 percent of Americans believe that fabricated news stories cause a great deal of confusion about basic facts—undermining public trust and eroding the quality of public discourse (Pew Research Center 2022).

The consequences go far beyond annoyance. As sensational content dominates feeds, echo chambers deepen. People are increasingly surrounded by information that aligns with their existing beliefs, making it harder to engage in meaningful, fact-based dialogue. In this climate, media is no longer a shared foundation for public understanding; it becomes a battlefield of competing realities.

Efforts to combat clickbait and low-quality content have included both technological and regulatory approaches. But momentum may be shifting. While platforms like Facebook and Google once invested in content moderation systems to demote low-quality content and surface authoritative sources, that posture appears to be changing. Facebook has recently announced it is stepping back from content moderation in news and political content, signaling a retreat from editorial responsibility. If more platforms follow suit, the problem could grow worse. Without safeguards in place, the ecosystem becomes even more vulnerable to misinformation, manipulation, and low-quality media designed to exploit rather than inform.

Even People Like You and Me Are Now Media

In the digital media world, even people like you and me are now integral parts of the ecosystem. While professional Creators and Influencers play a prominent role, the contributions of everyday users are equally vital. Social media platforms depend on our posts to monetize attention and generate revenue. In many ways, we are doing the work for them by creating content that keeps the digital world buzzing. Understanding the economics of attention helps us appreciate the value of every post and the significant role we all play in this media economy.

Everyday posts by regular users are the backbone of social media platforms. These posts range from sharing personal experiences, photos of family and friends, opinions on current events, to random thoughts and activities. While these posts may seem insignificant in isolation, collectively they generate enormous amounts of attention and engagement. Platforms like Instagram, TikTok, Facebook, and Snapchat serve as open channels, giving us the tools to publish and distribute content to our own networks and beyond.

And that content, however casual, is what drives the system. Every like, comment, share, and view contributes to the platform's overall activity, creating a rich tapestry of data that can be monetized. This behavioral data is invaluable for targeted advertising, which remains the primary revenue stream for most social media companies. Without the constant stream of user-generated content, these platforms would struggle to maintain engagement levels and, in turn, their profitability.

When you post a picture of your vacation or share a funny meme, you're not just connecting with friends and family—you're creating content that can be monetized. Platforms display ads alongside it, serve sponsored content into your feed, and use your engagement to refine algorithmic targeting. By sharing pieces of our lives online, we provide the raw material that these platforms need to attract advertisers. Every post—whether it's a carefully curated photo or a spontaneous status update—adds to the vast pool of content that keeps users coming back.

The power of everyday users in the media landscape should not be underestimated. While each of us may not have the scale or following of professional Creators, our collective impact is immense. Platforms rely heavily on the steady stream of content from millions of users to fuel engagement and revenue. In this way, everyday people are fulfilling the 3Cs of media: we use the Channel (social platforms), create the Content (our posts), and generate attention as both the Consumer and the product. We may not all be influencers, but in today's digital ecosystem, we all are media.

The 3Cs Revisited

We've covered a lot of ground in this chapter by surveying a diverse array of new players in the digital media landscape. Each has found a foothold in this environment by aligning with some combination of the 3Cs: Channel, Content, and Consumer. Let's now take a step back and observe the broader patterns.

Channels

Did you notice a pattern? Nearly every new player in this new media land leverages the opportunity to set up destinations on what we might call digital superhighways—platforms that are open to all. These shared, public spaces allow players to gain immediate reach and visibility. But what tends to distinguish today's media players is their use of proprietary channels— the spaces they control completely. This is where brands, retailers, and content providers can customize the environment, collect first-party data, and build deeper, more defensible relationships with their audiences. Proprietary channels aren't required to be in the media game, but they offer a level of control and ownership that public platforms alone cannot.

Content

The range of content flowing through this ecosystem is just as diverse as the players themselves. Some content is professionally produced and meticulously curated. Some content is tailored, personal, and community-driven in the Creator realm. Some content is developed with an alternative motive: whether to drive commerce, build a brand, or maximize click volume. And some content is shared incidentally by everyday people living their lives online.

All of this content comingles in the same feeds, search results, and platforms. It is this layering of content types—editorial, commercial, social, and opportunistic—that makes the digital media ecosystem both incredibly vibrant and increasingly difficult to navigate. But that's the nature of the system. Frictionless distribution allows everything to show up everywhere.

Consumers

Perhaps the most important shift of all is that the power is now in the hands of the consumer. With so many options at their fingertips, consumers have the freedom to build their media repertoires based on their own unique wants and needs. They can mix and match from a vast menu of content that can come from entertainment studios, news organizations, Creators, brands, retailers, or even friends and family. And because all of it is conveniently accessible on any digital device, the barriers to choice have all but disappeared.

The consumer is now the ultimate arbiter of what is useful. With limited time and attention, the decision to spend time with one form of media over another is consequential. Each player in this ecosystem must be driven by purpose: to fulfill the wants and needs of the audience better than all the alternatives available to them.

May the best content experience win.

5

The Rise of Platforms

As we venture deeper into the digital media age, it's crucial to understand how the various players fit into the broader media ecosystem. Today's media landscape is not merely a collection of isolated entities; it's a complex network of interconnected platforms. To truly appreciate where these players stand and how they interact, we must examine the underlying structure that supports the digital media world.

In the previous chapter, we observed that while some media players operate their own proprietary channels, many now rely on shared, public-facing platforms. This chapter will focus more closely on the structure of those platforms and the new power they wield in the media ecosystem. Rather than spotlighting individual players, we'll explore the overarching framework that connects them.

Imagine drawing a map of the digital media landscape: a network of nodes and hubs, each representing different media entities and their relationships to one another. This map reveals a pattern far more intricate and interconnected than the simpler, linear structures of the analog past. To make sense of this complexity, we turn to the principles of network science.

The digital media landscape is best understood as a scale-free network, where a few highly connected hubs dominate and countless smaller nodes orbit around them. These hubs are platforms that have risen to prominence. They are vital arteries through which information and content now flow. By examining how these platforms emerged, evolved, and established themselves as central to the media ecosystem, we gain insight into the dynamics at play in today's media environment.

Let's embark on a journey to understand the rise of platforms, beginning with a primer on network science and tracing the transformation from the analog era's isolated nodes to the interconnected hubs that now define the digital age. This chapter will illuminate how platforms have become the linchpins of the media landscape, reshaping how we access, share, and experience content today.

Network Science 101

If you're new to the world of network science, you may want to put this book aside for a moment and spend some time with Professor Albert-László Barabási. His seminal text, *Linked*, is by far the best description of the basics of network science that you could ever encounter (Barabási 2014). In this one text, you can go from a knowledge base of zero to being informed in ways that will help you not only understand the networked nature of media ecosystems but just about any other structure in life. You can also look for Professor Barabási on YouTube and watch one of his numerous talks, especially his visit to the MIT Media Lab, which is an oldie but a goodie!

The foundational ideas from network science—such as random networks, scale-free networks, and network resilience—help explain how power and influence are distributed in any system. In the sections that follow, we'll see how these concepts play out across media history, from the Newtonian Media Era's isolated nodes to today's platform-powered media hubs.

Before diving deeper, here's a quick-reference guide to several core terms from network science and how they apply to the structure of the digital media world. These concepts will anchor the analysis that follows and help you see why today's platforms function as dominant hubs.

Network Science 101
Network Science Terms That Explain How
Media Works Today

	Network Science Definition	Media Application
Node	A single point within a network that connects to other points. Nodes are the basic units that form networks.	A single media outlet, content creator, or distribution point within the media ecosystem
Hub	A node with a disproportionately large number of connections compared to other nodes in the network.	A media destination that houses many other content nodes that otherwise would be difficult to find on their own.
Random Network	A network where connections between nodes are made randomly, resulting in a relatively uniform distribution of links.	The Newtonian Media Era resembled a random network, with individual media companies operating mainly independently without dominant centralized hubs.
Scale-Free Network	A network characterized by a few highly connected hubs and many nodes with few connections, following a power-law distribution.	The modern digital media landscape resembles a scale-free network where individual content nodes operate mainly within platforms that act as dominant centralized hubs.

Network Science 101 (cont.)
Network Science Terms That Explain How Media Works Today

	Network Science Definition	Media Application
Fitness	A node's inherent attractiveness to gain connections based on its qualities or resources, influencing its likelihood of becoming a hub.	Platforms become dominant hubs due to their ability to execute their business models with excellence. They offer superior content and experiences that can attract and sustain audience attention.
Preferential Attachment	The tendency for nodes in a network to connect with already well-connected hubs, reinforcing their dominance.	Popular platforms grow faster because audiences are drawn to where other users already are, reinforcing their dominance.
Network Resilience	The ability of a network to remain functional despite the removal or failure of nodes, though failure of hubs causes major disruption.	Loss of a small media brand or individual content node has minimal impact but collapse of a hub can destabilize content discovery and access to audience attention.
Walled Garden	(Not a term in network science.)	A closed environment where a platform controls all content, user experience, and data, limiting outside access.

The Newtonian Media Map: A Study in Random Networks

In the Newtonian Media Era, the media map exhibited the characteristics of a random network. Back when there were fewer mass media, each media company—be it a television network, a radio station, a newspaper, or a magazine—existed as its own node that operated independently and thrived as a stand-alone entity. This system worked because channel capacity was limited, and audiences had fewer choices, leading to higher audience concentration around each node.

Still, even in this era of concentrated attention, it wasn't easy to get audiences to show up. A media brand going it alone had to work hard to earn awareness, build trust, and attract attention. It needed a large-enough scale to be viable and sufficient resources to promote itself. There wasn't a built-in discovery engine to surface content to the right people at the right time. If you were a niche player or wanted to take creative risks, the burden of visibility rested entirely on your shoulders. Every day was a battle for attention, with no algorithmic support and no centralized hub pointing audiences your way.

This is why economies of scale—a concept we'll revisit more fully in Chapter 10—mattered so much. Larger players could amortize the cost of content creation and promotion over a broader audience, while smaller outlets struggled to achieve sustainable reach. When choices were limited, it was easier to concentrate attention; but it still took effort, investment, and reputation to break through. Even with relatively little competition, there was no guarantee of being seen or heard.

However, even in this era, we began to see the early formation of platforms with the emergence of cable and satellite television and satellite radio. These mediums offered multiple channels and stations under a single distribution network, foreshadowing the platform phenomenon. Vertical stations or networks bundled together under cable or satellite providers illustrate the beginnings of a shift toward more interconnected systems where individual nodes started to rely on a shared infrastructure for survival. In essence, cable and satellite operating systems functioned like hubs in network science terms, and the network maps of these structures looked more like a scale-free network than a random network.

Importantly, this hub-like infrastructure enabled a new kind of media specialization. Television networks like ESPN (sports), MTV (music), CNN (news), and HGTV (home and lifestyle) could thrive alongside more general-interest broadcasters. These vertical channels were no longer constrained by the need to appeal to everyone at once. They could focus on specific audience interests—sports, music, home renovation, and the like—while benefiting from the aggregated distribution, promotion, and navigation tools provided by the cable or satellite operator. The same pattern held true in satellite radio, where listeners could find dedicated stations for jazz, heavy metal, stand-up comedy, political talk, or classical music—all curated with remarkable specificity.

This model was a win-win: content providers had the freedom to cater to niche tastes without needing to build scale alone, and audiences could explore deeper into their personal interests without friction. These early platforms gave rise to the idea that media could be both abundant and targeted. This idea would later define the digital era; but here, it was still underpinned by curated, centralized control.

The Digital Media Map: A Study in Scale-Free Networks

With the digital revolution came an exponential expansion in media supply, and the network topology transformed dramatically as a result. Unlike the random networks of the analog era, digital media networks are characterized by a few highly connected hubs—platforms—that control the flow of information and content within and across an almost unimaginable number of nodes. Just like what we witnessed with cable and satellite television and satellite radio, there was no way for all these individual nodes to survive on their own. These platforms became crucial because without them, it would be incredibly difficult for audiences to discover and access individual nodes in such a fragmented environment.

This phenomenon is partly explained by the "long tail" effect, where a vast number of niche content pieces exist alongside a smaller number of popular ones (Anderson 2006). In a highly fragmented network, the likelihood of a niche node (or less popular content) being discovered is low unless it is connected to a platform that can aggregate and recommend it to the right audience.

Understanding the necessity of hubs in this highly fragmented network helps explain why platforms have become so central to the digital media ecosystem. Without these hubs, the sheer volume and diversity of content would make it nearly impossible for users to navigate and for content creators to reach their audience. Platforms like Google, Facebook, Apple, and Amazon, among others, emerged as these critical hubs, using sophisticated algorithms and vast amounts of user data to facilitate discovery and engagement. They provide the necessary infrastructure for connecting users with content, ensuring that even the most niche nodes can be found.

This role of platforms as hubs is essential for the survival of individual nodes as they offer a way to manage the overwhelming abundance of content and connect it with the appropriate audience. Furthermore, platforms don't just serve as conduits; they also curate and recommend content, enhancing user experience and engagement. They leverage the principles of fitness and preferential attachment from network science— whereby the most connected nodes continue to gain more connections, further solidifying their status as hubs. This creates a positive feedback loop that reinforces the importance and dominance of these platforms in the digital media landscape.

The Evolution of Platforms into Walled Gardens

What's most interesting about some of the largest platforms that dominate the digital media terrain today is that they didn't necessarily start out as platforms whose primary function is to serve as an operating system for all the nodes that are housed within it. Platforms like Facebook, Google, YouTube, Apple, Amazon, X (formerly Twitter), Instagram, and TikTok began as specific services but evolved into comprehensive ecosystems. Each platform originally served a unique function: Facebook was a social network, Google an aggregator/search engine, YouTube a UGC

(User-Generated Content) video channel, Apple a hardware and software company, Amazon an online retailer, X a news feed, Instagram a photo-sharing site, and TikTok a burgeoning video platform in China. Over time, these platforms expanded their services, integrating various types of content and functionalities and transformed into what are now referred to as Walled Gardens.

The Role and Utility of Walled Gardens

Walled Gardens are distinct from traditional network hubs because they erect barriers that contain user experiences within their ecosystems. The term "Walled Garden" originates from the idea of a space enclosed by high walls. Nothing enters or exits without the owner's permission. In digital media, Walled Gardens refer to platforms that tightly control the user experience, data, and content within their boundaries, deliberately restricting access to external services and sources.

This containment strategy is driven by the value of the audiences and the first-party data generated through engagement within these walls. Platforms like Facebook, Google, Amazon, and others function as Walled Gardens by creating self-contained environments that users rarely need to leave. Facebook, for instance, not only hosts social interactions but also offers news, video, and marketplace content which then ensures prolonged engagement. Amazon has created a similarly immersive experience, where you can stream premium video and shop for virtually anything without ever leaving its ecosystem. For every Walled Garden, there's a comparable story.

What makes these Walled Gardens especially unique is not just their infrastructure but the unprecedented convergence of content types within them. Editorial, commercial, branded, creator-made, and even everyday user content now coexist within the same interface—often within the same feed. The boundaries between content sources have dissolved, creating an environment where every piece of content, regardless of its origin or intent, competes on equal footing for audience attention.

In network science terms, Walled Gardens differ from traditional hubs, where bridges often connect different nodes and enable a freer flow of information across the network. In contrast, Walled Gardens intentionally limit or eliminate these bridges, keeping audiences and data inside. This structure maximizes user retention and engagement, ensures total control over data, and creates a significant competitive advantage by making it harder for users to switch to other platforms.

The implications of this model are significant. While these platforms offer unprecedented access, personalization, and convenience, that access comes with trade-offs. The consumer is no longer just the beneficiary of expanded choice; they have become the product, the data source, and, increasingly, the captive. What feels like freedom may in fact be a carefully engineered experience that becomes difficult to exit. In these closed-loop ecosystems, consumers often fail to realize how constrained their choices have become.

For advertisers, the rich first-party data within Walled Gardens is incredibly valuable, but access is tightly controlled by the platforms themselves. This dynamic creates a powerful incentive for both users and content creators to stay within the Walled Garden, further reinforcing the platform's dominance and solidifying its role as a critical hub in the digital media landscape.

Can Nodes Survive Outside of a Platform?

Can any node survive outside of a platform? That's where branding comes in. Only a few strong transmedia brands can thrive independently. All other media require some form of platform structure to host them. This insight helps explain the general health of various media sectors in the digital realm. Those sectors that remain disintermediated face more significant challenges than those that have consolidated into hubs.

Let's look at the newspaper industry. A few powerful brands are doing fine on their own. But the rest, who must operate as individual nodes in what remains a more randomized network, are struggling. That's why platforms like Google News are so compelling to the newspaper industry. Google News provides a hub for content created by newspapers that struggle to find their audience.

This insight also explains why the structure of streaming television is evolving before our eyes. Individual streaming networks, which can be considered platforms in their own right, realize it's hard to profit by going alone. Hence, the great re-bundling of streaming services has begun.

Today, we see strategic alliances between streaming services such as Disney+, Hulu, and ESPN+ among others. The larger the hub, the better in this highly competitive and fragmented streaming television world.

We see this phenomenon in other sectors as well. The radio/audio industry is dominated by platforms in satellite distribution, digital streaming, and digital/over-the-air broadcast. Magazine media have consolidated under publishing ownership groups to recognize the economies of scale of multi-title ecosystems. Even out-of-home media has consolidated into major ownership groups that can create scale from each individual location under their purview.

Can Platforms Become Too Powerful?

As we take a step back and consider the topography of the digital media landscape, we must ask ourselves whether these platforms serve an essential purpose or whether they are becoming too powerful. In network science terms, platforms serve as essential hubs. Without them, the diverse nodes of content and users would not be able to connect and thrive. A certain degree of consolidation is necessary to provide the content diversity that digital media offers.

However, if a platform becomes too powerful and too restrictive, it poses significant problems. Some argue that certain platforms behave more like utilities than media. A utility is an essential public good that is regulated to ensure it operates in the public interest. When platforms wield power with their first-party data and build powerful algorithms to suit their vested interests, we should all be concerned. For instance, platforms like Facebook and Google have faced scrutiny for their data practices and market dominance, raising questions about their influence on public discourse and competition.

Regulatory bodies are increasingly monitoring these platforms, considering measures to ensure they do not stifle competition or manipulate information to their advantage. Consumers are also impacted by the growing power of platforms, facing concerns about privacy, data security, and the availability of diverse content.

Ultimately, there's a difference between the structure of the media and the behavior of players within that structure. Platforms, while essential, must be held accountable to ensure they do not misuse their power. We're going to dedicate an entire section of this book to the business of the media business because it's that important. Understanding the balance between the necessity of platforms as hubs and the danger of their potential overreach is crucial for navigating the future of digital media.

What Happens When Platforms Fail?

Network science doesn't just help us understand how platforms rise; it also explains how they can fall.

In a scale-free network, most nodes can fail without disrupting the overall structure. But if a hub collapses, whether through external attack or internal failure, the entire network can destabilize. This is what makes the role of platforms so critical and, at times, so precarious.

You've probably heard the phrase "too big to fail"—an expression that gained prominence during the 2008 financial crisis to describe large institutions whose collapse would have devastating ripple effects on the broader economy. The same concern now applies to digital platforms. When a dominant hub in our media ecosystem falters, it doesn't just affect the company—it disrupts how audiences discover content, how creators get visibility, and how advertisers reach people. The stakes are high.

We may be on the precipice of such a moment. The US government is actively pursuing antitrust action to break up Google's dominance across advertising and search. At the same time, the AI arms race is reshaping the landscape, potentially reordering which platforms rise to the top. Having hub status today does not guarantee platform supremacy tomorrow. We've seen this story before: early internet users once relied on Yahoo, Lycos, or AltaVista to navigate the web until Google's model overtook them. As Barabási (2014) notes, in networked systems, newer, fitter nodes can quickly unseat those that once seemed invincible.

If today's platforms falter through regulation, competition, or technological shifts, network science suggests that new hubs will rise to take their place. The structure will persist, even if the players change.

The random networks of the Newtonian Media Era are gone. In their place, we now have a media galaxy so vast that its stars—individual nodes—can no longer shine in isolation. They need the structure of a constellation to stand out. Platforms are that structure. Whether today's platforms maintain their gravitational pull or give way to a new generation, the hub-and-node architecture of digital media is here to stay.

6

Digital Media's New Gold

In the previous chapter, you learned about the platforms that create the underlying structure for all the nodes in the digital media ecosystem. These platforms have also become a treasure trove of first-party audience data. What exactly is first-party audience data? Why is it so important? In this chapter, we will explain the rise of first-party audience data and how it has become a game changer in the digital media world. We could go so far as to call it "Digital Media's New Gold."

Why Is Audience Data so Valuable?

To understand the value of first-party audience data, you first need to understand the vital role that audience measurement data plays for media companies. Audience measurement data underpins the valuation of both the media company's content and audience products. Media companies need to measure "who" and "how many" people are showing up at any given point in time to engage with content on the media company's channel. This serves a dual purpose: first, it helps content creators get to know their audience, which informs the creation and refinement of content to better meet their preferences and needs. Second, it helps identify and quantify the audience for the purpose of selling time and space to advertisers who wish to engage with audiences that match their consumer profiles.

Media companies analyze audience measurement data to understand what content resonates most with their audience. They can identify patterns and trends—such as which genres, topics, or formats are most popular at different times. This helps them tailor their content strategy to match audience interests. For example, if a particular type of content sees a spike in engagement, the company might invest more in producing similar content to keep the audience engaged. Data-driven insights enable the development of personalized content recommendations. Platforms can use sophisticated algorithms to recommend content based on an individual's history and preferences. This personalization keeps audiences engaged longer and encourages them to explore even more content on the channel. By leveraging audience data for personalization, media companies can increase loyalty and satisfaction. And garnering loyalty is key when audiences have too many choices and only a fixed amount of attention to allocate to all those choices.

Now, let's turn to the valuation of the audience product for the purposes of generating advertising revenue (for those media companies who are ad-supported). By measuring "who" and "how many" people are engaging with their content, media companies can use this information to negotiate advertising pricing with marketers who wish to place their ads on the media company's channel. Advertising rates are set based upon the desirability of the audience to the advertiser—how closely they represent the characteristics of the advertiser's customers—and how many can be reached. Importantly, advertisers are willing to pay a premium to reach a targeted and engaged audience. This data enables more precise audience targeting, which can increase the effectiveness and value of advertising placements. Knowing a wide range of audience demographics and behaviors is key to optimizing revenue streams from advertising.

Finally, media audience measurement data fuels a media company's business strategy. Media companies are interested in knowing all types of demographic and behavioral characteristics of their audiences. The more they know about them, the better they can understand them—not just as media consumers but as real people with real lives. Each media brand must understand how they fit into their audience's media repertoires and how they stack up relative to the competition. Media companies then use this information to carve a position for themselves in the marketplace for marketing to existing consumers and to grow their audience base. In marketing terms, we call this STP—segmentation, targeting, and positioning. In essence, it defines your market opportunity by serving specific consumer segments better than the other available choices in the marketplace. By knowing your audience's sweet spot, you can grow by catering to both existing customers and those who are "look-alikes" of the customers you already have.

Different Measurement Methods for Different Times

Media audience measurement was vastly different back in the Newtonian Media World. First, the unique structure of each form of media required its own measurement methods. Independent third-party measurement providers rose in prominence to create a common measurement standard in a particular media sector. The beauty of this third-party measurement system was that it was objective and uniform. All parties abided by the same standards and the same units of measurement. In essence, media audience measurement back in the day created a "common currency" that could apply to any and all media within a particular sector.

Who were these independent third-party measurement providers? Ever heard of A.C. Nielsen? They were (and still are) responsible for measuring and publishing audience ratings for television. Later in the history of this era, they acquired a company called Arbitron and they became responsible for measuring radio audiences as well. Nielsen also dabbled in website measurement. But they weren't the dominant player in the early days of digital media during this period of history. A company called Comscore rose in prominence as the dominant internet audience measurement provider. In print media, we had the Audit Bureau of Circulation (ABC) and later the Alliance for Audited Media (AAM) to audit circulation while another research house known as Mediamark Research (now known as MRI-Simmons) was the preferred provider for measuring magazine audiences. And out-of-home media was measured by the former Traffic Audit Bureau (TAB).

Each provider used methodologies to measure and report audience metrics that made sense for the medium. Television published "ratings" while websites published "traffic" and "unique visitors." Magazines published circulation and "readers per copy," and so on. What we were left with is what we refer to as "apples and oranges." From a methodological standpoint, it was impossible to combine these measures to create a holistic view of an audience's media consumption across media forms.

While each media sector had its own unique methodology, they all shared something in common: they all relied upon panel data. The significance of panel-based measurement lies in its approach to estimating audience behavior. Panels require a representative sample of the population for the purpose of auditing media consumption. The data from these panels were extrapolated to provide insights into broader audience trends. This method was practical given the technological limitations of the time, but it also meant that audience measurement was based on estimates derived from a relatively small sample of users. This panel-based approach would later become an issue as media capacity expanded in the digital era. The size of these panels would have to grow exponentially in order to accurately measure all the activity across the digital media landscape.

These independent measurement providers were not just operating in isolation. They were regulated by groups of media companies and advertisers who formed committees and councils to oversee and audit their methodologies. In the United States, organizations like the Media Rating Council (MRC) played a key role in reviewing and accrediting measurement systems. This regulation was crucial in ensuring that the data provided was credible and reliable. The methodologies used by these providers had to be open to scrutiny, which involved rigorous audits and validation processes. This transparency allowed all parties involved to trust the data being used in their financial decisions.

During this period of our media history, the audience measures were based upon broad demographics. This was partly due to limitations in the measurement methodologies that required statistically viable panels. But the beauty of using broad demographics is that the view of the audience was relatively the same for any media company and any potential advertiser who was evaluating the size and composition of the media company's audience product. While we all acknowledge that broad demographics do not paint the most accurate picture of individuals with their idiosyncrasies, they do a good job of defining audience segments en masse. Remember, during this period, the media were considered "mass" media, and we were more concerned with scale than with precision. It was a different time, and the metrics that came along with it suited the period.

Digital Leaves a Rich Data Trail

As we transitioned from analog to digital media, audience measurement changed significantly. Due to the structure of digital media, we can measure just about anything and everything! Unlike traditional media, where audience measurement relies heavily on panel data—sampling a small, representative group to estimate broader behavior—digital media can leverage both panel data and census data. Census data involves the comprehensive collection of information from every user interaction across digital platforms, without the need for sampling. This is possible because digital media operates on platforms that can capture detailed records of every click, scroll, and interaction. Every time a user engages with digital content, a data point is recorded, creating a rich, continuous stream of information. Over time, as these data points accumulate, they form a detailed profile of each user, tracking everything from their browsing habits and content preferences to the times they are most active online. This ability to collect data at the individual level, across vast audiences, enables a depth and precision in audience measurement that was unimaginable in the analog era.

You may have heard the term "cookies" in relation to your online activities. Cookies are small text files stored on your device by websites you visit, and they play a pivotal role in measuring audiences in the digital media realm by helping websites remember you and track your behavior across the web. There are two main types of cookies: first-party and third-party. First-party cookies are created and stored by the website you're visiting directly, enabling the site to remember your preferences, such as login details or language settings, providing a more personalized experience. Third-party cookies, on the other hand, are created by domains other than the one you're currently visiting, and they require the website's authorization to be placed on your device. These cookies track your behavior across multiple websites, building a profile of your interests and activities over time. The key difference is that first-party cookies are generally used to enhance the user experience on a single site, while third-party cookies are employed to gather broader data across multiple digital destinations.

Regulators Aren't Kind to Certain Forms of Measurement

As digital media has evolved, so too has controversy surrounding the ways in which audience behavior is tracked and measured. Third-party cookies, in particular, have come under intense scrutiny. While these cookies have been instrumental in enabling advertisers to target specific audiences with remarkable precision, they have also raised significant privacy concerns. The ability to track users across multiple websites, often without their explicit consent or full understanding, has led to a growing unease among consumers and regulators alike. This concern has given rise to stringent regulations aimed at protecting user privacy, with the California Online Privacy Protection Act (CalOPPA) and the General Data Protection Regulation (GDPR) being two of the most prominent examples. These regulations require companies to be transparent about their data collection practices, obtain user consent before collecting personal data, and provide users with the ability to control their data. The intent behind these laws is clear: to curb the excesses of digital tracking and give individuals more control over their online privacy.

However, compliance with these regulations has been challenging for many in the industry, particularly when it comes to third-party cookies. The very nature of these cookies makes it difficult to ensure full transparency and user control. This has led to a broader push within the industry to move away from third-party cookies altogether. Big Tech companies, most notably Google, announced plans to phase out third-party cookies in favor of new, privacy-compliant alternatives. Yet, despite the fanfare, these efforts have been marked by repeated delays and growing skepticism. The transition away from third- party cookies has proven to be more complex than anticipated, with concerns about how it will impact advertisers and the broader digital economy. Although we've been talking about third-party cookies going away for years now, they're still here.

In response to these challenges, Big Tech is developing what some have termed "black boxes"—new methods of tracking and targeting users that aim to comply with privacy regulations while still offering the precision that advertisers demand. Google's proposed Privacy Sandbox is one such example (Google 2025), where user data is processed within the browser itself, and only aggregated insights are shared with advertisers. These solutions are designed to protect individual user identities while still allowing for targeted advertising, though critics argue that they simply shift the balance of power further into the hands of the tech giants. The outcome of these efforts remains to be seen, but what is clear is that the landscape of digital audience measurement is undergoing a significant transformation, driven by a mix of regulatory pressure and technological innovation.

First-Party Data Emerges as Digital Media's New Gold

As the digital media landscape grapples with increasing privacy concerns and stringent regulations, first-party audience data has emerged as a crucial asset. In an environment where third-party cookies are under scrutiny and consumer demands for privacy are at an all-time high, media companies are finding themselves more reliant on the data they collect directly from their own users. This shift back to first-party data is not just a matter of compliance; it's a strategic response to the evolving digital ecosystem. This data enables companies to build a deeper, more personalized relationship with their users, fostering loyalty and engagement in ways that are both meaningful and more privacy-compliant.

This shift in the value of data has also transformed the role of digital media channels themselves. Historically, the media landscape, as described by Professor Philip Napoli's (2003) dual product marketplace, derived economic value from two primary products: content and audience. The channels that delivered this content were seen as necessary instruments, facilitating the connection between the two but not generating direct value themselves. However, the rise of first-party audience data has fundamentally altered this dynamic. Channels are no longer just delivery systems; they have become valuable assets in their own right.

In many ways, the increasing importance of first-party data reflects a broader shift in how digital media companies think about value. First-party audience measurement data has become the foundation for understanding and anticipating audience needs. This has led to a scenario where it can now be viewed as "digital media's new gold"—a resource so valuable that it underpins entire business models. Companies that can effectively harness this data stand to gain a significant advantage in the digital media world where user trust and regulatory compliance are paramount.

Media Audience Measurement 101
The People, the Methods, and the Data Behind Audience Measurement

	Definition	Application to Media Audience Measurement
Different Views of the Audience		
Demographics	Statistical characteristics of a population, such as age, gender, income, and education.	Used to define audience segments en masse and enable common currency across media sectors.
Advanced Audience Characteristics	Audience traits beyond demographics, including attitudes, preferences, lifestyles, and behavioral tendencies.	Helps media companies and marketers understand audiences not just as media consumers, but as real people with real lives.
Online Behaviors	Observable actions taken by individuals in digital environments, including clicks, views, scrolling, and sharing activities.	Helps media companies and marketers anticipate what audiences want based upon their past behaviors. Serves to guide recommendations.
Past Purchase Behaviors	Data reflecting previous purchasing decisions or transaction histories of individuals or groups.	Past purchase behaviors can be used to predict the likelihood of purchase in the future. Mainly used by marketers for ad targeting.

Media Audience Measurement 101
The People, the Methods, and the Data Behind
Audience Measurement

	Definition	Application to Media Audience Measurement
Audience Measurement Methods		
Panel Data	Audience data collected from a representative sample, extrapolated to estimate behaviors of the broader population.	Traditional "currency" for TV, radio, and print; also used in cross-platform tracking efforts.
Census Data	Audience data collected from the entire population or total user actions without sampling.	Common in digital media, where all user interactions are logged at scale.
Audience Data Sources		
First-Party Data	Data collected directly by an organization from its own users through owned digital properties or platforms.	Increasingly valued due to privacy regulations and its ability to power personalization and loyalty strategies.
Second-Party Data	First-party data shared with a partner organization via direct agreement.	Common in data-sharing agreements between retailers and media companies.
Third-Party Data	Data aggregated by entities without a direct relationship with the individual, often sourced across multiple outlets.	Creates a sorely lacking "common currency" across digital media domains. At direct odds with first-party audience data.

Are We Any Better Off Today?

For all the advancements we've made in collecting precise, granular audience data within individual platforms, we've lost ground in understanding the whole audience across platforms. Back in the Newtonian Media Era, our challenge was methodological. We were trying to compare "apples and oranges" due to the technical constraints of different analog channels. Each medium had its own third-party measurement system, its own terminology, and its own standards. But even with those limitations, we had some semblance of transparency and consistency. Everyone used the same common currency within each channel, and the data, while broad, could be trusted and interpreted in relation to adjacent media types.

Fast forward to today, we find ourselves in the era of Convergence. In theory, this should have solved our historical problems. After all, if content can now travel across screens and devices seamlessly, shouldn't our measurement systems do the same? Ironically, the opposite is true. The more granular and domain-specific our measurement has become, the more fragmented our view of the total audience. First-party data may be rich and precise; but by definition, it is siloed. What a consumer does on Amazon is invisible to what they do on *The New York Times*. What's happening inside Meta's ecosystem has no bearing on what happens within YouTube or Netflix. Each platform has an extraordinary view of its own audience, but that view doesn't travel.

The result? A measurement arms race is underway. Cross-platform panels attempt to fill in the gaps, and various industry alliances are trying to establish new forms of currency. Some believe the internet service providers—those who carry the traffic for all these platforms—may be in the best position to connect the dots. But so far, no one has fully cracked the code. We have more data than ever before, and yet we still can't build a truly holistic view of how audiences move across content, devices, and time. We've gained precision at the cost of perspective. Whether that trade-off was worth it remains an open and urgent question.

Will Data Overshadow the 3Cs?

Our understanding of audience data in the digital media world has evolved significantly since the earlier editions of *Media: From Chaos to Clarity*. Back then, we referred to this data as "digital exhaust," a term reflecting our uncertainty about its value and purpose. Today, things have certainly changed.

Media audience measurement data, particularly first-party data, now plays a crucial role in understanding who, what, where, when, and how audiences engage with content within specific digital channels.

This information drives every decision we make, from shaping content strategies to crafting audience profiles for digital advertising campaigns. This shift leads us to ponder a critical question: Has data itself become more valuable than the content that initially draws the audience?

Historically, we built the media foundation on the 3Cs. Yet, there is currently no place for "D"—the data that increasingly drives media strategies—in this acronym. This raises an existential question: Should data be integrated into the very framework of media? If so, how might this disrupt the foundational relationship between audiences and the content they seek?

There is no dispute that data matters. Without a clear understanding of how each C is performing, media companies are essentially flying blind. Data is an invaluable diagnostic resource. It illuminates and illustrates. But when it begins to overshadow what it sets out to measure, we're all in trouble.

The sacred relationship is between media and the audiences they serve. Audiences care about convenient, efficient, and affordable access to content that serves their wants and needs. If data helps to facilitate that, so be it! But when data becomes the key ingredient to unlocking revenue potential, it's hard to maintain the proper perspective. While data is undeniably vital to the business side of media, it isn't (nor should it be) the core business product itself.

Should data be digital media's new gold? It shouldn't. The better path is to remain steadfast in our commitment to the 3Cs and ensure that data supports rather than supplants the sacred relationship between Content, Consumers, and the Channels that bring them both together.

7

The Struggle for Clarity Continues

Welcome to the digital world. Over the past six chapters, we have explored how media evolved from analog systems into today's digitally networked ecosystem. That backstory was essential to understanding the landscape we now inhabit. But now that we're here, a new question emerges: Are we done?

Not even close.

In the first two editions of *Media: From Chaos to Clarity*, the journey was the story. We were living through transformational shifts. We were watching new technologies redefine the roles of channels, which in turn reshaped how content was created and how consumers engaged. But that chapter is now closed. The analog-to-digital transition is complete. We live in a digital world.

And yet, the journey continues.

New technologies arrive daily, each one promising to change everything. The pace of change hasn't slowed; it's simply taken a new form. So how do we make sense of it all? How do we know what matters and what is just noise?

That's what this chapter is here to help with.

It's about sharpening your instincts. It's about learning to distinguish the transformational from the trivial. Because if there's one thing the digital era has taught us, it's that distraction is everywhere. And clarity? That's something we still have to fight for.

Even in its relative youth, the digital landscape is already littered with failed innovations that once dazzled and then disappeared. To navigate what comes next, we need to understand the difference between three types of innovation: fads, mainstream trends, and evergreen shifts.

Fads flare up suddenly—briefly capturing attention before fading fast. Everyone wants in when they're hot, but they rarely leave anything lasting behind. Mainstream innovations take a slower path: they begin with early adopters, gain traction, and eventually enter the cultural norm. But even these can lose their shine as the next big thing arrives. Evergreen innovations are different. Once they take hold, they endure—adapting, evolving, and remaining relevant over time.

Knowing how to spot the difference is essential for navigating a media world that never stops moving.

The Metaverse: A Case Study in Shiny Objects

If you need a case study in how easily shiny objects can capture imaginations, look no further than the Metaverse.

On October 28, 2021, Mark Zuckerberg announced that Facebook would become Meta, signaling a bold pivot from social networking to a vision of an immersive virtual universe. The promise was sweeping: a fully integrated digital realm where people could live, work, and play through virtual and augmented realities. It was pitched not as an add-on to our social media experience but as a wholesale replacement for it.

The rebrand made headlines around the world. That very day, a media strategy professor in Chicago (yours truly) appeared on the local evening news, raising doubts about the dramatic shift. The skepticism wasn't rooted in cynicism but in pattern recognition and practical experience. Was the public really clamoring to live in a fully virtual world? Maybe a niche segment, yes. But for most people, digital media supplements physical life; it doesn't replace it. The concept felt familiar, echoing an earlier chapter in digital experimentation known as *Second Life*. That platform faded into obscurity for a reason.

Beyond the consumer lens, there was a glaring business problem. Was Zuckerberg truly prepared to walk away from Facebook's cash-printing advertising business model in favor of a still-theoretical virtual realm? The infrastructure wasn't ready. The audience wasn't ready. And the business case was shaky at best. It felt less like a pivot and more like a house of cards that was stacked on hype with little to support it.

Still, for a moment, the Metaverse became the center of gravity in the tech and business worlds. Consulting firms flooded our email inboxes with weekly Metaverse reports. Brand marketers rushed to launch virtual storefronts and claim digital real estate. The narrative wasn't just speculative; it was breathless.

But the core disconnect came down to a misalignment between technology and mindset. The hardware was expensive and clunky, but more importantly, the public wasn't asking to substitute real life with simulation. People use digital tools to enhance their lived experiences—not escape them.

And then there's the business model. Transitioning from an ad-supported social platform to a capital-intensive, immersive ecosystem wasn't something that could happen overnight. The economics didn't pencil out. And as the buzz faded, so did the funding. Reports disappeared. Platforms were quietly repurposed, downsized, or shelved even when the name "Meta" remained.

Still, the story remains valuable. Not because the Metaverse succeeded; but precisely because it didn't. For innovation to stick, it must marry mindset with execution. It must be useful, usable, and desirable at scale.

That's the lesson of the shiny object: beware the dazzle that distracts from reality.

The Mindset Test

How can we anticipate the future without falling into the trap of shiny objects that often sweep us off course? The failure of the Metaverse offers an important clue. The technology was cumbersome, and the audience wasn't ready for it. For any innovation to take hold, it requires more than just a flashy debut. It demands the marriage of mindset and technology. Only when people's mindsets align with technological advancements can a new idea reach its full potential in the media world.

So what do we mean by mindset?

At its core, mindset starts with the audience. In the 3Cs paradigm, the Consumer C is foundational. If a technology does not align with the way people think, feel, and behave—if it doesn't enhance life in meaningful and intuitive ways—it simply won't gain traction. Media theorist Marshall McLuhan addressed this in his *Laws of Media* (McLuhan and McLuhan 1988), particularly the law of enhancement: new technologies must offer a clear benefit over what already exists. They must improve upon familiar capabilities in ways that feel natural and worthwhile. If that enhancement isn't immediately recognizable or if the technology creates friction instead of removing it, audiences will reject it.

This was one of the core problems with the Metaverse. It failed to offer a compelling enhancement for most people's lives. The idea of replacing the physical world with a virtual one didn't align with how the broader population wanted to live. And even for those willing to engage, the user experience was clunky, inaccessible, and difficult to integrate into daily routines. In other words, the technology failed to meet the moment—and the mindset.

Different Mindsets among Different Media Generations

Understanding mindset means knowing who the intended audience is and how they perceive the world. This is crucial because for any technology to succeed, it must align with the lives of the people it's meant to serve. Technology must do more than exist; it must enhance daily life in ways that are both meaningful and intuitive. But to predict how people will adopt new innovations, we also need to explore an important factor: generational orientation toward media.

We are all, in many ways, byproducts of the media landscapes that existed during our formative years. As explained by Professors Martin Block and Don Schultz (2009) in their book *Media Generations*, the media that surrounded us during our teen years shapes how we understand and engage with future technologies. For example, Baby Boomers, who grew up in a world of mass broadcast media, may see new technology through a different lens than Gen Z, who grew up immersed in social and interactive digital media. These generational differences play a profound role in determining how new innovations are received, and whether they ever become mainstream.

But these generational mindsets don't operate on just one level. They shape and are shaped by multiple dimensions of consumer experience. At the individual level, people develop personal habits, expectations, and emotional connections to media: what feels familiar, what earns trust, and what adds value to everyday life. At the community level, media use becomes social and normative, driven by group practices, peer adoption, and collective rituals that define what "we all use." And at the cultural level, entire generations reflect shared values and symbolic meanings around media—whether it's the role of journalism in democracy, the meaning of privacy, or the social capital tied to platform use.

Does this mean that older media generations cannot adapt to emerging technologies? Not at all. Instead, they become immigrants in a new media paradigm, with varying degrees of assimilation depending on personal choice. The decision to adopt new technology often depends on its perceived utility: if it offers clear value and is accessible, adoption becomes more likely.

That said, each media generation does have its preferences. Social media platforms offer a prime example of this. Over the relatively short history of social media, a clear pattern has emerged: each generation gravitates toward different platforms. Ask a teenager today if they spend much time on Facebook, and they'll likely tell you that Facebook is where their grandparents hang out (Pew Research Center 2023).

As we continue to navigate this evolving media landscape, we must ask: Who is this innovation for, and how will it fit into their lives? Will it reach them at a time when their technological preferences are already set? Or will it become the new normal for a younger generation?

Regardless of where the change begins, the key question remains: How does this innovation make life better for the people it serves across individual habits, community practices, and cultural beliefs? If the benefits aren't clear across these levels, the technology risks being abandoned along the side of the road as we move forward in this ever-changing media world.

Scaling Innovation: The Broader Mindsets That Matter

While the consumer is the central figure in the marriage of mindset and technology, innovation doesn't reach scale on audience adoption alone.

For any idea to take hold across the media ecosystem, other stakeholder mindsets must also come into alignment, especially those responsible for sustaining and commercializing media at scale.

Media companies must determine whether the innovation supports their editorial mission, distribution goals, and operational realities. It's not just about whether the audience is present; it's whether the innovation allows them to serve that audience better, more efficiently, or more profitably. In the chapters ahead, we'll examine the pressures media companies face in balancing legacy structures with new capabilities and how these tensions often slow adoption or distort execution.

Marketers who invest resources in advertising must evaluate whether a new technology helps them achieve their objectives: whether that's building brand equity, driving short-term sales, or targeting a more precise audience. If a platform or format doesn't demonstrate a clear communication advantage or measurable impact, marketers will hesitate to invest. In an era increasingly driven by attribution and performance metrics, innovations that don't fit into existing marketing implementation and measurement systems often struggle to gain support.

In addition to these three core stakeholders, we have to consider the role of investors. Investors look for evidence of future value—scalable growth, defensible advantages, and market viability. If an innovation doesn't point toward a clear business model or if its adoption requires substantial unproven behavior change, investor enthusiasm fades. They want to fund ideas with traction, not just potential.

Furthermore, content creators—a group that now spans from traditional producers to independent influencers—must feel that the technology empowers their creative goals. If it adds friction, complexity, or compromises their connection to the audience, they may opt out. The creator mindset is often overlooked in the innovation cycle; but it's essential. Without engaged creators producing meaningful content, even the most advanced platform will struggle to hold attention.

In this way, the business model isn't a separate layer tacked on after innovation; it's a direct reflection of these collective mindsets. If any piece is out of sync, the system stalls. When everything aligns—audience need, strategic fit, creative potential, and commercial viability—momentum builds.

That's why some innovations scale and others don't. And it's why shiny objects are so alluring: they often gain attention before alignment takes place. In the chapters ahead, we'll use this broader lens to explore the state of the media business today—where stakeholder mindsets are not always in sync, where chaos continues to emerge, and where the search for sustainable value remains unfinished.

Marriage of Mindset & Technology
Distinguish Meaningful Innovation from Shiny Objects

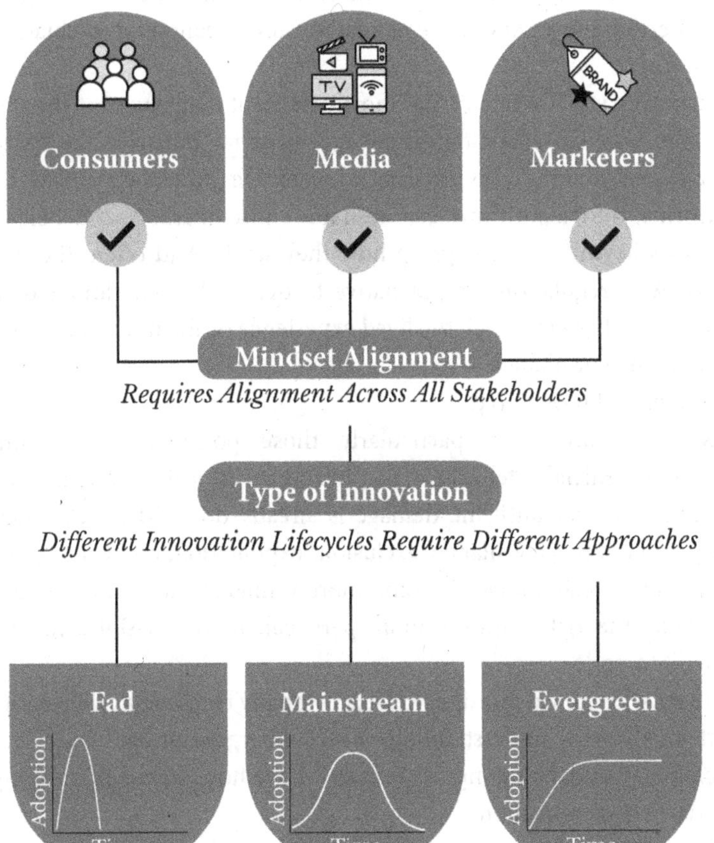

Regulatory Challenges and Ethical Accountability

As we consider the marriage of mindset and technology, we must also ask a deeper question: What guardrails are needed to protect the relationship? Innovation doesn't exist in a vacuum; it operates within the lives of real people, and those lives can be enriched, exploited, or even harmed by the media systems we build.

It's easy to focus on enhancement. Much harder, but equally important, is asking: What could go wrong? What are the unintended consequences? Where might exploitation or inequity take root? These questions are not afterthoughts; they are essential to any meaningful evaluation of innovation.

Regulatory lag is one of the most persistent challenges of the digital era. The pace of technological advancement far outstrips the speed at which governments can legislate and enforce protections. New tools, platforms, and algorithms can reshape entire markets and behaviors before policymakers fully grasp how they work. And often, the people tasked with regulation are not native to the media generations driving innovation. They may lack the lived experience or fluency required to act with urgency or nuance.

But we still have to try.

Media technologies, particularly those powered by algorithms, data, and artificial intelligence, can introduce ethical dilemmas that are difficult to detect until the damage is already done. These can include misinformation, surveillance, exclusion, exploitation, and even systemic bias. And as technologies become more immersive and embedded into daily life, the risks become more personal, more invisible, and more difficult to undo.

That's why ethical foresight must accompany technological innovation. And that's why understanding—deep, intergenerational, and cross-disciplinary understanding—is required if we hope to create meaningful standards and protections.

The essential question is not merely whether the technology can scale but whether it should. Who stands to benefit? Who might be left behind? And who bears the risk?

Mindset and Technology in Harmony

As we reflect on the lessons of this chapter, one message becomes clear: in this ever-evolving media landscape, success lies not in chasing the latest shiny objects but in understanding how mindset and technology must work together in harmony. While innovation will always captivate our imaginations, not all of it will stand the test of time. To discern which technologies will truly shape our future, we must stay grounded in the needs and desires of the people they aim to serve.

It all begins with understanding mindsets: knowing the media generations and their unique orientations toward new technology. Each innovation must seamlessly fit into the lives of its intended audience by enhancing daily routines in ways that are meaningful, intuitive, and accessible. Technology, at its best, should be so effortless that it feels like an extension of ourselves.

For any new media innovation to thrive, it must be more than just functional; it must offer real value to those who embrace it. That's the true test: Does this technology serve us, improve us, or make our lives better in some way? If it does, it stands a chance of becoming a lasting part of our daily lives. If not, it will likely fade away. A relic of the past, left behind as we continue our journey.

And that journey isn't over. In fact, it never will be. We don't know exactly where we're headed, but by keeping our eyes open to the powerful union of mindset and technology, we can begin to anticipate which innovations will take root and which will simply come and go. The future will undoubtedly surprise us, but by embracing this framework, we can navigate chaos with a clearer sense of purpose. Who knows what the next edition of this book will have to say? Only time will tell if our predictions were right. But one thing is certain: the marriage of mindset and technology will continue to shape our world, just as it always has.

Part II

And Back, Again: Welcome to Chaos Once More

Prelude: What to Expect in Part II

Part I brought us through the journey from the order of the analog media world to the full arrival of digital media in all its complexity. But now that we've landed, we must confront an uncomfortable truth: just because the digital transition is complete doesn't mean clarity has prevailed.

Part II takes us into the business side of media—and it's here where the cracks really begin to show. If Part I explains how we got here, Part II reveals what's happening now behind the scenes: a media industry under pressure, with fundamentals that no longer work the way they once did.

This section begins with a grounding in the fundamentals. Chapter 8 introduces three building blocks of the media business: the attention economy, the design of effective business models, and the structure of marketplaces that enable the exchange of value. These concepts help set the foundation for what's to come.

In Chapter 9, we observe a significant shift in how media functions within the broader economy. What was once a business centered around audience attention is now increasingly a means to drive commerce. We explore how content and advertising have blurred into shoppable experiences and how media companies risk becoming tools in someone else's transaction model.

Chapters 10 and 11 reveal the breakdowns in other key components of the business model. Chapter 10 reflects on the loss of scale that once enabled media companies to thrive. Without mass audiences, it becomes harder to amortize content costs, serve advertiser needs efficiently, or foster shared cultural experiences. Then, in Chapter 11, we turn to the fraying relationship between media companies and marketers. Once reliable allies, marketers are now narrowing their focus to owned audiences and performance metrics, leaving media companies to monetize the margins.

Chapter 12 expands the view from relationships to systems. Here, we examine the rise of programmatic advertising and how complexity bias has introduced inefficiency and opacity into the marketplace. What was once a promise of precision has become a convoluted web that favors intermediaries more than the content creators or advertisers themselves.

We close this section with Chapter 13, which asks a timely and essential question: Are media companies still delivering on their side of the value exchange? Using a customer-centric lens, we revisit the pillars of meaningful audience service—offering solutions, relevant information, true value, and accessible experiences—and consider whether today's media businesses are truly living up to them.

Part II isn't just about what's broken. It's about recognizing how we got here and why the pressure points we see now are not random—they're the natural result of fundamental shifts in how value is created and captured in the digital media economy.

8

The Fundamentals of the Media Business

Before diving into all the woes that the media business faces today, it's important to get grounded in the fundamentals of the media business. That's what this chapter is all about. First, we're going to question what business the media are ultimately in by unraveling the tangled web of supply and demand. Next, we'll look at how individual businesses operate by studying their business models through the lens of the 3Cs framework. And finally, we'll introduce the marketplaces that bring buyers and sellers together in the media economy. What could possibly go wrong? Plenty! But to understand all the problems that are unfolding before our eyes, we first need a good grounding in business fundamentals.

The Tangled Web of Supply and Demand

Any business can be explained by the basic principles of supply and demand. One party has something to offer, another wants it, and price is determined where the two meet. If something is in limited supply and high demand, the price tends to rise. Conversely, if something is widely available and few people want it, the price typically falls. The outcome needs to work for both parties. Both have to benefit from the exchange. We call this reciprocal value creation.

Media companies operate on the supply side of the equation. They produce and distribute content to serve the wants, needs, and desired experiences of audiences who become consumers of that content. Audiences, then, are on the demand side of the equation. They want convenient and affordable access to content that suits their needs at any given point in time. Therefore, price is set at the intersection of media supply and consumer demand, right?

If only it were that simple. The perceived value of the content, the availability of alternatives, and the quality of the delivery channel all influence what the audience is willing to give in the exchange. Sometimes the audience will pay directly for access, and other times they pay with a different form of currency: their attention.

As described by Professor Philip Napoli's (2003) *Dual Product Marketplace*, media are suppliers of content that creates the supply of a second product: audience attention. If a media company chooses, they can offer audience attention for sale to advertisers to help fund their operations. In these cases, we can welcome another participant in the supply and demand exchange: advertisers who are investors in the media economy to gain efficient access to audience attention.

And the attention economy is big business. According to Professor James Webster (2014), audience attention is both scarce and fragmented. In a world of media abundance, attention becomes the limiting factor and therefore one of the most valuable assets in the entire ecosystem. When audience attention is concentrated within ad-supported media environments, it can be monetized. But when attention is directed to other forms of media that do not include advertising in the business model, it is lost.

Remember that prices are set at the intersection of supply and demand. And as you'll soon find out, content supply is expanding far beyond any consumer's willingness to pay for all of it. And while demand for attention may still be there, marketers are finding new ways to circumvent the system to engage directly with consumers. It leaves us with a tangled web of supply and demand dynamics that we'll unpack in the coming chapters.

Understanding How Media Companies Operate

With this general understanding of the media business and its supply and demand dynamics, let's shift our focus to how individual media companies build their businesses and operate within the system. To evaluate any business, it's essential to understand the dynamics of the business model driving it. A business model is essentially a framework that outlines how a company creates, delivers, and captures value.

This chapter uses the 3Cs framework as a foundation for understanding the key components of media business models. The 3Cs can explain how reciprocal value is created by delivering content to consumers through various channels. These three elements independently and collectively shape the core operations of any media company.

And like any "for-profit" business model, media companies must be able to operate as efficiently as possible and be able to grow without sacrificing performance or increasing expenses at the same rate.

Let's take a closer look at each component of the model.

Consumers

Identifying and valuing "who" your business is for is the crucial first step in any business model. Everything begins with the consumer. The process starts by segmenting the market—carefully defining various groups and determining where one group ends and another begins. Once an audience segment is clearly defined, the next step is to size it: Is the audience large enough to sustain the business, or is it a smaller niche with high-value potential? Valuation follows. Some audiences are willing to pay for content directly, while others are more valuable because their attention is valuable to advertisers. Understanding both payment potential and advertiser interest is essential. Only after a segment has been identified, defined, sized, and valued can media companies decide whether it's worth pursuing.

A successful business must then understand the consumer segments they intend to pursue deeply. In the case of the media business, that means going beyond basic demographics to uncover motivations, values, media behaviors, content preferences, and contextual life patterns. Persona building is a valuable tool in this process. It helps transform research and insights into strategic action by creating detailed, human-centered representations of key consumer segments that drive the media company's success.

The deeper the understanding, the more tailored and resonant the business strategy can be. Only then can media companies begin to build and deliver upon a promise to their consumers. And that promise is the fuel that brings the business model to life.

Content

Once a company has gone through the rigorous process of identifying, sizing, valuing, and deeply understanding its audience, it can then turn its sights toward developing its content strategy. Content production and distribution decisions aren't made in a vacuum. They're led by a North Star that is often referred to as a value proposition. A value proposition is the promise a company makes to its consumers: what value it will deliver, how it will do so, and why it's worth choosing over alternatives. This promise is the foundational link to the consumer relationship and defines how trust, loyalty, and long-term engagement will be earned. In today's oversaturated media ecosystem, a media company must live up to its value proposition with every piece of content it distributes.

Value propositions can take many forms, depending on the type of media company and its consumer base. For example, a streaming service might offer a vast and diverse library of content, available on demand, as its core value proposition in order to appeal to audiences seeking convenience and variety. A niche publication might focus on delivering highly specialized content that caters to a specific interest or industry, promising depth and expertise that general media outlets cannot match. Social media platforms, on the other hand, might offer the value of connection and community to enable users to share, engage, and interact with content and each other in meaningful ways.

A successful value proposition goes beyond merely offering content; it must resonate with the audience's values, preferences, and lifestyle. It should clearly articulate why consumers should choose this media company over others by emphasizing the unique advantages and experiences it provides (Peck and Malthouse 2010). Whether the company is focused on entertainment, education, community building, or any other type of content, the value proposition must align with the audience's needs and be consistently delivered. This alignment fosters trust and loyalty, positioning the media company as the go-to source within its niche or market segment.

While every piece of content that a media company distributes must live up to the company's value proposition, not all forms of content hold the same economic value for a media company. Content can be classified across three tiers: premium, parity, and commodity (Franks, Malthouse, and Maslowska 2024). Premium content is highly valued by the audience and difficult to find elsewhere. Consequently, consumers are likely to pay directly for it. Parity content belongs to a broader category, such as shows available across competing streaming services. It holds value, but the audience knows there are alternatives. Commodity content, by contrast, is widely available and easily duplicated. Audiences are generally unwilling to pay for it, and the viable path to monetization is often through advertising.

Does that mean that only premium content can fuel a healthy business model? Not necessarily. Content can be very expensive to produce (or acquire from someone else). Content that costs a lot to produce and distribute requires a different revenue model than content that is readily available at limited to no acquisition costs. In today's media ecosystem, there are business models that support all three content tiers successfully.

Channels

Regardless of which content tier a media company operates in, all face a new challenge brought on by the forces of Convergence and open circuits. Media companies rely on some degree of exclusivity to build a viable revenue model. But Convergence has blurred the lines between media channels, and open circuits allow content to travel freely across platforms whenever an engaged audience member chooses to share it. This dynamic poses a serious challenge to content control and monetization strategies and sets the stage for the final "C" in the 3Cs framework: Channel.

In the Newtonian Media Era, a media company's business model was often defined by its primary mode of distribution. Each channel carried its own infrastructure, regulatory environment, and cost structure. These differences shaped how media companies operated, how they reached audiences, and how they made money. Channels also acted as natural boundaries between competitors. But Convergence has erased many of those boundaries. Today, companies that once operated in entirely different spaces are now bumping into one another, all competing for the same scarce audience attention.

Most media companies today operate what we'll refer to as a home channel: a proprietary environment they control, such as a website, mobile app, or owned streaming platform. At the same time, they distribute content on public platforms that are available to almost anyone, including social media and third-party aggregators. This dual-channel approach presents both advantages and challenges.

Home channels allow companies to manage the user experience, collect first-party data, and monetize engagement more directly. But they also require significant investment in technology and user experience. Public platforms, on the other hand, offer scale and visibility; but they often limit control over the user experience and restrict access to meaningful audience data.

Channel strategies also vary depending on the format. Some channels require licenses such as those operating on the broadcast spectrum. Others demand licensing agreements with gatekeepers like cable providers, satellite distributors, and streaming hubs. Out-of-home media channels often involve leased real estate and must comply with local governance and zoning laws. And print media involve significant production overhead costs and physical distribution networks that are both cumbersome and expensive.

Regardless of the channel type, one thing remains constant: audiences expect not just content but an intuitive, accessible, and respectful user experience. That means content must be easy to find and enjoy, and the platform must function smoothly without crossing any lines when it comes to data usage or privacy. A strong channel strategy doesn't just deliver content; it strengthens the brand's value proposition and reinforces its relationship with the audience.

The Financial Model Has to Work

Now that we've examined how media businesses operate through the lens of the 3Cs, we can turn to the financial model—which translates those strategic components into revenue and cost structures that sustain the business.

Revenue

In the context of business models, a "revenue stream" refers to the specific sources of income a company generates through its operations. A strong and reliable revenue stream is widely understood to be sustainable, predictable, and scalable. Sustainability ensures that the revenue remains viable over the long term. Predictability allows companies to anticipate future cash flow with reasonable confidence, and scalability indicates that revenue can grow in tandem with the company's expansion.

Revenue generation can be understood through the interplay of the 3Cs. Content itself can be a direct revenue stream. Media companies may charge audiences for access through subscriptions or microtransactions. Alternatively, they may earn income by licensing or syndicating their content—charging other entities for the rights to distribute it on different platforms or in different markets. In both cases, the content product holds intrinsic value and serves as a primary source of economic return.

Consumers also play a direct role in revenue generation, particularly in ad-supported models. When audiences engage with content, media companies monetize that attention by selling access to advertisers. The more engaged and well-defined the audience, the more valuable the opportunity. Some companies may also generate revenue from the consumer data associated with that attention, though privacy regulations have begun to shift those dynamics.

Channels, too, now play a more prominent economic role. Historically, channels served as distribution pathways with little inherent value outside the content they carried. But in today's environment, digital channels are often destinations themselves. Audiences sometimes pay for the convenience of aggregated content, and platforms may generate revenue through subscription fees, tiered access models, or integration with commerce experiences. Channels can also become revenue hubs that share income with creators whose work attracts large-scale audience engagement.

Media companies that build revenue strategies across all three Cs are better equipped to adapt to changing market conditions and to sustain long-term growth. Diversification across these areas helps stabilize income, reduces dependency on any one stream, and allows media businesses to remain resilient in a rapidly shifting ecosystem.

Cost Structures

With the revenue side of the equation under our belts, let's now turn to the costs. Cost structures define the expenses a company incurs to create, deliver, and support its products or services. These costs can be categorized into fixed and variable costs. Fixed costs are expenses that remain consistent regardless of the level of production or sales. Variable costs, on the other hand, fluctuate with the level of production or output. General accounting principles guide how these costs are allocated, ensuring they align with revenue generation and reflect the true financial position of the company.

Using our 3Cs definition of media, costs can be broadly categorized into three main areas: content, channels, and customer relationships. Costs associated with content include expenses for creating, acquiring, and producing content, whether it's video, audio, written content, or interactive experiences. Channel-related costs involve maintaining and enhancing the platforms or distribution channels through which content is delivered to the audience, such as technology infrastructure and user experience design. Customer relationship costs cover the expenses of engaging with audiences and advertisers, including marketing and sales efforts aimed at attracting and retaining viewers and ad buyers.

Different media companies have different cost structures based on the type of content they produce and/or distribute, the channels they use, and how they market to their audiences. For instance, a company focused on high-end, original video content will have a vastly different cost structure from one that aggregates third-party content or user-generated content. Companies operating primarily on digital platforms may incur higher technology costs but lower physical distribution costs. These variations influence how media companies approach scalability and growth, making it essential to tailor cost management strategies to their specific business models.

Fostering Partnerships to Get the Job Done

Sometimes media companies are sole operators, going alone to forge meaningful relationships with consumers. Other times, they form strategic partnerships to achieve their goals. These alliances enable companies to collaborate in ways that benefit both parties. Strategic partnerships can take many forms such as: joint ventures, licensing agreements, or technology collaborations. They are often aimed at leveraging each partner's strengths to achieve shared objectives. By pooling resources, sharing expertise, and accessing new markets, partnerships help companies enhance their capabilities, reduce costs, and accelerate growth. They are a key component of business models across industries, and in media, they're often what make it possible to deliver on the promise of the 3Cs.

In the media industry, partnerships are particularly crucial because of the multifaceted nature of content development, channel management, and customer relationship strategy. Each area demands specialized expertise that often lies outside the core capabilities of any single organization. Content development requires creative collaborators such as writers, producers, designers, and editors who bring stories to life across formats. Channel requirements call for partners who can handle licensing, platform optimization, infrastructure management, user experience, and audience data management. And in today's attention economy, customer relationship management has become just as critical. It depends on data scientists and audience strategists who can personalize experiences and optimize engagement to foster long-term loyalty.

The orientation of a media company—whether it leads with Content, Channel, or Consumer—significantly influences its approach to strategic partnerships. These alliances aren't just about strengthening core capabilities; they help fill gaps where a company may lack in-house expertise. A business focused on premium content production, for instance, may rely on partners to power its distribution channels and unlock audience insights. A company built around channels and user experience may look to content creators or research firms to round out its offering and better serve its consumers. By partnering strategically, media companies can build more resilient and adaptive business models that are better equipped to compete and evolve in a dynamic, converging ecosystem.

Media Companies Operate in a Cluttered Marketplace

No media business operates in isolation. Business models are proven based upon their ability to compete for attention, resources, and relevance in a crowded marketplace. The media landscape is a highly competitive environment where companies must continually distinguish themselves. Healthy competition drives innovation, pushing media companies to refine their content, improve user experiences, and better serve their audiences.

However, in an era of content overload, the risk of market saturation is real. Audiences are inundated with choices, and too much competition can lead to fragmentation, making it increasingly difficult for any one company to capture and maintain a loyal consumer base. This underscores the importance of competitive differentiation as a foundational element of a media company's strategy, influencing everything from audience targeting to content development and distribution.

Understanding the competitive landscape means recognizing that media companies are no longer just competing within their traditional categories. Thanks to the forces of Convergence, they now face competition across multiple channels and content types. A media company might find itself competing with streaming services, social media platforms, linear broadcasters, and even individual content creators, all vying for the same audience. Therefore, knowing your competitive set—both direct and indirect competitors—is essential.

By continually assessing and responding to this competitive context, media companies can better differentiate themselves. They must ensure that their value proposition stands out and remains relevant in an ever-evolving marketplace. Competitive differentiation, the unique attributes that set a media company apart, is critical to ensuring that offerings resonate in an already crowded market. It's not just about knowing who your consumer is and what they value; it's about understanding the competitive forces that also vie for their attention and strategically positioning your business within that landscape.

Figure Out How to Grow

Scalability is a critical component of any business model. It refers to a company's ability to grow and manage increased demand without compromising performance or efficiency. A scalable business can expand its operations, its customer base, and/or its product offerings with minimal incremental costs, often achieving what is known as "economies of scale." This means that as the company grows, the cost per unit of output decreases, making growth more profitable. Scalability typically involves leveraging technology, optimizing processes, and building systems that can handle increased volume. For companies across industries, scalability is essential for achieving sustainable growth and maintaining a competitive edge in rapidly changing markets.

In the media industry, scalability remains crucial even in a landscape that has shifted away from mass media. While media consumption is now fragmented across countless niches, the need for scale has not diminished. A media company that serves a niche audience must still efficiently manage its growth by ensuring that as more audiences discover and engage with its content, it can handle the increased capacity without degradation in quality or service. This reflects a core principle from network science: if a media destination is "fit," it attracts more connections, and the more connections it has, the greater its potential for continued growth. Scale, then, isn't just a business objective—it's a structural advantage in networked systems.

Scalability should be assessed across all three Cs. On the content side, media companies must find ways to efficiently increase output while maintaining quality. For channels, it involves ensuring that distribution networks can handle larger volumes of content and users without bottlenecks. Finally, customer relationship management must scale to effectively engage and support a growing audience base, potentially through strategic partnerships that bring in the necessary expertise or technology. By addressing scalability across these areas, media companies can adapt to increasing demands and remain competitive in a dynamic marketplace.

Marketplaces Facilitate Exchange among Players

So far, we've focused on what media companies produce, how they deliver it, and how they capture value. But how do they actually sell their wares to interested buyers? That's where marketplaces come in. In economic terms, a marketplace is, at its core, a system or environment where buyers and sellers interact to exchange goods, services, or information. It's a dynamic space where supply meets demand, with prices typically determined by the interaction of these forces. In any marketplace, the goal is to bring together those who have something to offer with those who are seeking to acquire it, facilitating trade, competition, and economic growth.

In the context of the media industry, marketplaces operate on multiple levels, each with its own unique dynamics. The two most prominent media marketplaces are those that connect audiences with media companies and those that connect advertisers with media companies. In some instances, the audience will transact directly with a single media company, while in others, the audience will engage with a platform that aggregates content from various suppliers. Sometimes the audience will pay a subscription fee or a microtransaction fee for access, while in other instances, the audience will pay indirectly with their attention that is then monetized with advertising revenue.

The second type of marketplace in media is the interaction between advertisers and media companies. This marketplace is centered around the monetization of audience attention. Here, media companies sell access to their audiences to advertisers who are willing to pay to reach these potential customers. The rise of digital platforms has significantly transformed this marketplace. Today, transactions often occur in real time through automated systems like demand-side platforms (DSPs) and supply-side platforms (SSPs), enabling advertisers to bid for ad space in milliseconds based on the specific audience segments they want to reach. We refer to this type of marketplace as a programmatic marketplace.

What Could Go Wrong?

At first glance, the fundamentals of the media business appear solid. Media create valuable content and deliver it through channels that reach audiences. They generate revenue by monetizing that connection either through audience payments, advertiser support, or some combination of both. But as you've seen in this chapter, the model is more complex than it appears. Maintaining equilibrium across the 3Cs requires precision. There are multiple interlocking parts that must work in harmony for the business to thrive.

And yet, harmony has become harder to come by.

The digital realm has not merely disrupted this system; it has introduced a level of chaos unlike anything we've seen before. Business models are under pressure. Long-standing relationships are strained. And the very foundations that once held the media ecosystem together are now shifting beneath our feet.

What follows isn't a simple unraveling; it's a series of stress fractures across every layer of the media business. Each one reveals how hard it is to sustain the fundamentals in today's environment and how much is at stake if we fail.

9

Media as a Means to a Different End

For decades, the media business was built around a sacred relationship: one between the media company and the audience it served. The audience was meant to be at the center of everything: the primary customer. Advertisers, while essential to fund the system, were always intended to be secondary. Their interests were to be accommodated but not allowed to overpower the media company's content strategy or consumer experience.

But when so much of the media economy depends on advertising, the balance of power is always at risk. This wasn't as much of an issue when advertisers were primarily concerned with access to audience attention. Today, advertisers are no longer satisfied with simply paying for access to attention. They want more, and digital media has the capability to deliver it. Advertisers seek the ability to directly link their advertising investments to the sales of their products and services.

The media business model appears to be shifting right before our eyes into what is now referred to as a "content-to-commerce" model. As a result, the narrative is shifting from media's sacred relationship with its audience to media's role in a different story—the story of commerce. Media is becoming a means to a different end.

The Evolution of the Business Model: From Attention to Transactions

As media has evolved, so too have the components of the business model that drive transactions between advertisers and media companies. This evolution can be understood in three distinct phases—V1.0, V2.0, and V3.0—each representing a shift in how value is exchanged and measured within the media ecosystem.

V1.0: The Era of Attention and Opportunities to See

In the earliest stage, V1.0, advertisers paid media companies for access to audience attention, and the primary metrics were gross audience impressions along with the measures of reach and frequency. This was a straightforward model that was focused on creating opportunities to see—the simple act of placing an ad in front of as many eyeballs (or ears) as possible. The value exchange was clear: media companies provided access to audiences, and advertisers paid media companies based upon the estimated number of potential exposures to their ads. However, the impact of these exposures was less certain. Advertisers had to model the relationship between exposure and sales independently. They often relied on imprecise marketing mix modelling. There were many unaccounted-for steps in the customer journey, and much was left to chance. This left advertisers to bridge the gap between the opportunity and its outcome.

V2.0: The Rise of Direct Response

As digital media began to take hold, the business model evolved into V2.0, characterized by the integration of a direct response (DR) approach. In this phase, value was no longer just about exposure; it was about action. Advertisers and media companies began trading value based on specific audience actions, such as clicking on an ad or visiting a website. While direct response had been used in the analog era, particularly to sell off less desirable inventory, it became central to early digital advertising. This model provided a sense of security in the new and uncertain digital advertising environment, as advertisers paid only for measurable actions. However, the challenge of linking these actions to actual sales—known as attribution—remained complex and often elusive. The rise of clickbait farms, discussed earlier, further muddied the waters by generating clicks without meaningful conversions.

V3.0: The Seamless Integration of Content and Commerce

Today, we are in the V3.0 phase, where the media–advertiser relationship has transformed into a seamless integration of content and commerce. In this model, the content itself is often shoppable; thereby collapsing the entire customer journey into a single, unified transaction. Audiences can now engage with content and purchase what they like on the spot, eliminating the need to leave the platform or visit another destination. This shift has fundamentally altered the business model, making media not just a means of capturing attention, but a direct facilitator of transactions. The once-separate worlds of content and commerce have converged, reflecting a new era where media's role in driving sales is immediate and direct.

Evolution of the Media Business Model

This table summarizes the key changes across V1.0, V2.0, and V3.0 phases of the media business model

	V1.0: Attention & Opportunity to See	V2.0: Rise of Direct Response	V3.0: Seamless Integration of Content and Commerce
Primary Business Model Focus	Access to audience attention	Driving measurable audience actions	Facilitating seamless content-to-commerce transactions
Basis of Value Exchange	Payment for potential exposures (reach and frequency)	Payment based on audience actions (e.g., clicks, visits)	Payment based on direct purchases or completed transactions
Type of Transaction Measured	Audience exposure	Audience actions	Completed purchase transactions
Content's Role	Capture attention and build audience relationships	Prompt immediate audience actions	Collapse the journey into shoppable content, integrating commerce
Consumer Behavior – Media Consumption	Passive consumption of content	Interactive consumption designed to trigger action	Active engagement with content as a shopping experience
Consumer Behavior – Actions on Advertising	Minimal tracking beyond exposure	Measured through direct clicks and visits	Direct pathways from content to purchase without leaving platform
Consumer Behavior – Purchase Behavior	Disconnected from media consumption, measured	Loosely connected via action metrics, attribution remains complex	Fully integrated purchase behavior, collapsing discovery and transaction
Channel Responsibility	Delivering audience attention for advertisers	Delivering audience actions (clicks, visits)	Acting as a commerce arm facilitating direct transactions

Who Is Best Positioned to Take Advantage of Content-to-Commerce?

As the media business model continues to evolve toward seamless integration between content and commerce, the question arises: Who is best positioned to capitalize on this shift?

Surprisingly, it's not the legacy media companies that once dominated the landscape. Despite their expertise in creating and distributing content, these media companies lack the critical infrastructure needed to compete in the content-to-commerce model. Two essential components—first-party customer data and a robust commerce platform—are missing. Without these assets, they struggle to adapt to a world where media isn't just about generating attention but about facilitating transactions.

The Rise of Retail Media Networks (RMNs)

In contrast, retailers, especially those with vast e-commerce infrastructures, capitalized on this opportunity. They didn't need to be traditional media companies; they simply needed content that could be monetized through seamless, shoppable experiences. The result was the rise of Retail Media Networks—a new breed of digital media platforms built and operated by retailers who now wield incredible power in the media landscape. Unlike legacy media, the RMN model is built on product sales. Imagine the marriage of first-party customer data for product purchases with first-party audience data on the media these customers consume. It's a match made in heaven! Retail Media Networks enable its advertisers to track a customer's journey from ad exposure to purchase in real time. It collapses the once-complex path from awareness to transaction into a seamless process.

Who are some of the largest RMNs? They're well-known retailers such as Amazon, Walmart, Kroger, and Target among many others. As reported by *Adweek*, Amazon's advertising revenue soared to $56 billion in 2024 (Johnson 2025). Retail advertising spending in the United States is projected to swell to nearly one-quarter of all ad spending in the United States by 2028 (Lebow 2024), placing even more pressure on traditional media companies to adapt or risk losing their share of the market.

Social Network Platforms Join the Game

The rise of content-to-commerce isn't confined to retailers alone. Social network platforms like Instagram, Facebook, and TikTok quickly developed commerce arms to get in on the action.

Instagram, for example, has integrated features like Instagram Shopping, where users can purchase products directly from their feed or stories without ever leaving the app. This makes it possible for Marketers and Creators to create visually engaging, interactive content that can immediately convert to sales, all within the ecosystem of a social media platform.

Social platforms already have one advantage: they were designed for user engagement and audience interaction. Adding a commerce layer felt like a natural extension of their business model. By combining the rich, visual nature of their platforms with seamless shopping experiences, these companies are redefining the line between social interaction and commerce. For marketers, this means another high-engagement platform to directly sell products and services to consumers.

New Players with Different Objectives

Consider all these players who are now in the content-to-commerce space. They are part of the media ecosystem as they have built a 3Cs paradigm—they use their retail channels to deliver shoppable content to consumers who happen to be their retail customers. But, are they truly media companies whose primary focus is the media business?

When you look up "Who we are" on Amazon's website, you will notice they do list entertainment among their core business offerings (Amazon n.d.). But, it's just one of many service offerings that include a focus on retail, web services, artificial intelligence, devices, and operations. Jeff Bezos understood the strategic value of integrating media properties such as MGM, Twitch, and their own Prime Video streaming service into its Walled Garden. Remember, content creates attention that can then be harvested with advertising. And in Amazon's case, the advertising can link directly to sales through Amazon. In essence, Amazon creates "closed loop attribution"—a one-stop experience for advertisers.

What about Walmart? How do they define themselves and how do they talk about Walmart Connect as part of their business strategy? As Rich Lehrfeld, SVP and GM of Walmart Connect, explained in a company blog post, "At Walmart Connect, we exist to create meaningful connections between our customers and the brands that matter most to them. For customers, this means new experiences to discover the right products at the right time to save money and live better. For brands, we help boost their visibility and ways to grow with Walmart" (Lehrfeld 2024). Does this at all resemble the media fundamentals and essence of the media business model that was outlined in the last chapter? No. Walmart Connect exists to facilitate retail—as it should.

What about Kroger, Target, or Macy's? How do they talk about their retail media operations? Do you notice a trend here? Instead of media being the core business, it serves another purpose that has little to nothing to do with the traditional foundations of media and the sacred relationship between the content consumption experience and its audience. Media is clearly a means to a different end.

No One Has a Trifecta in the Content-to-Commerce Game

We are witnessing a content-to-commerce arms race. The question becomes who will get there faster? Will retailers learn the tricks of the media trade? Or, will media companies who aren't saddled with the baggage of brick-and-mortar retail thrive in the digital commerce space?

While new players who are not squarely focused on media now find themselves in the media business, they often can't do it alone. The content-to-commerce model requires three core ingredients: great content that can attract audiences and hold their attention, robust first-party data that can facilitate the advertising-to-sale attribution process, and an e-commerce platform to fulfill orders. When you consider the players in the content-to-commerce space, each is lacking in at least one of these key ingredients. That's where legacy media companies enter the fray.

Given these dynamics, strategic alliances between media companies and retailers could offer a solution that leverages the strengths of both. Retailers bring data and infrastructure, while media companies bring content and audience engagement. Together, they could create powerful content-to-commerce experiences that neither could achieve alone. These partnerships could take many forms, from co-branded content to shared data strategies that allow for more personalized shopping experiences. The key is to find a balance that allows media to retain its integrity and value as a content provider while also benefiting from the revenue potential of commerce.

Some legacy media companies are forging partnerships with RMNs to leverage their content production capabilities in exchange for a share of the revenue generated from transactions. For example, in 2021, Meredith Corporation (now part of Dotdash Meredith) partnered with Walmart's Retail Media Network to create shoppable content (Nasdaq 2021). Similarly, NBCUniversal has worked with retailers like Walmart to integrate shoppable ads across their streaming platforms, including Peacock (Wood 2023). Through these partnerships, NBCUniversal provides premium content that connects audiences directly with products featured in shows, movies, or ads, allowing viewers to make purchases in real time. These are just two examples among a myriad of partnerships that are emerging between legacy media companies and retail partners.

Importantly, as e-commerce fulfillment becomes increasingly accessible, media companies, if they choose, can build commerce integrations directly into their own platforms. Instead of outsourcing their content to retailers to help make their retail media channels stronger, they can keep the content on their own channels and outsource back-end fulfillment. Take *New York Magazine*'s "The Strategist" as an example. In this instance, the trust built between the brand and its readers creates a perfect extension for e-commerce that "The Strategist" offers. In essence, *New York Magazine* has created a digital catalog filled with products that are recommended by the editorial team. It's a stamp of credibility, and the audience can shop directly from the media brand's digital platform. In fact, most major magazine publishers have embraced shoppable editorial strategies to make it easy for their readers to buy what they like directly from the page.

Will Content-to-Commerce Ultimately Strengthen or Weaken the Media Business?

The rise of content-to-commerce business models can either be a good thing for the media business or it can cause major problems for it. The future depends upon the following factors: whether the players reinvest resources back into the core offerings that media provides, whether advertisers realize that not all advertising should be transactional, and whether media companies remain squarely focused on the relationship between its content and the audience.

Beware of the Marketing Loss

The content-to-commerce model can either be a savior or it can destroy the media business model. It all depends upon whether media is treated as a marketing loss or whether media is strengthened by the new resources generated by these other business models. When media becomes secondary to another business objective, it often shifts focus away from the core purpose of producing and delivering content to suit the wants, needs, and experiences of the audience. Instead, the media becomes a tool for achieving other goals, such as selling the products and services of advertisers.

In business terms, this situation can lead to what's known as a "marketing loss." A marketing loss occurs when a product or service, instead of being an end in itself, becomes a means to support another business goal. Consider the canonical example of a grocery store that puts milk on sale to draw customers into the store. While the milk is sold at a loss, the end goal is the profit made by the shopper's entire basket. When media is used in this way, the original value proposition can be diluted, leading to a loss of focus on the relationship between content and its audience.

We should raise a red flag when businesses that do not consider themselves to be in the media business take resources out of the media economy without reinvesting the resources and expertise back into the core offering that media provides. Do these companies have the expertise to manage their media operations? Are resources flowing back into the production and distribution of high-quality content? Does the content delivered on these channels serve the wants and needs of the audience, or are there other masters being served?

On the other hand, the infusion of commerce into content could provide much-needed funding for high-quality journalism and entertainment, allowing media companies to thrive in a digital economy where ad revenues are increasingly hard to come by. Despite these challenges, there is potential for a more positive outcome if resources from these ancillary business models are reinvested back into media operations. With additional funding, media companies could produce more engaging, diverse, and high-quality content, enriching the overall media ecosystem. As content costs are amortized across broader business scenarios, consumers may enjoy more affordable access to a wide range of media offerings.

Beware of Advertising That Focuses Solely on the Sale

Advertisers play a role in determining the fate of this story. In their quest for chasing a perfect correlation between advertising expenditures and sales, they may very well destroy how advertising is supposed to work across the entire customer journey, from top to bottom.

Unfortunately, we are living in an era of hyper accountability where every advertising expenditure is held accountable to immediate sales. This short-termism can become a book unto itself.

If advertisers lose sight of their brand-building efforts and the role of pure-play media companies in helping them to situate their brands in culture, they will not only dilute their businesses, but they will take the ad-supported media business down with them. As more advertising revenue shifts away from traditional media business models and into the content-to-commerce models that are dominated by retailers, something or someone needs to compensate for these losses.

Where can new sources of revenue come from? Audiences can only pay so much for the media they enjoy. They can't make up for the losses in advertising revenue. Subscription fatigue is such a profound issue that we'll address it in a coming chapter. So if audiences can't pay much more, who can? Some news media outlets are now relying upon donations from foundations and other non-profit business models to keep them afloat. The entire media industry cannot take advantage of a non-profit model. It may work for news and critical information, but it doesn't fit the entertainment services of many media companies.

The reality is that the future of the media industry business model needs viable advertising support to fuel it. And that advertising needs to work in ways that include commerce but also embrace some of the older versions of the advertising business model. Perhaps instead of an evolution from V1.0 to V2.0 and V3.0, we need a combination of all three models to sustain both advertisers and media companies.

Beware of Serving the Wrong Customer

As content-to-commerce grows, the lines between editorial content and advertising are becoming increasingly blurred. Shoppable editorial content is designed to engage audiences while also offering them the opportunity to purchase the products featured in the content. This can enhance the user experience by making it more interactive and personalized, but it also raises questions about the integrity of the media. Advertorials and native advertising have long existed as forms of content that blend editorial and advertising. However, with content-to-commerce, this blending becomes even more pronounced. In some cases, what appears to be genuine editorial content is, in reality, an advertisement designed to drive sales. This raises ethical concerns about transparency and the potential for consumer deception.

There is a risk that media could be reduced to a mere marketing tool, valued not for its content but for its ability to drive sales. If the fundamental relationship between media and its audience is lost, media will lose its raison d'être, and we'll all suffer for it. The advertiser is not the primary customer; the audience is the ultimate consumer. The advertiser benefits from a healthy media–audience relationship, and the integrity of that relationship must be maintained at all costs. That means delivering content and experiences that audiences want—not what advertisers will pay for. It's a fine line that can't be crossed.

Will We Be Better Off?

As we have explored throughout this chapter, the media landscape is undergoing a transformative shift toward a content-to-commerce model, where media not only informs and entertains but also acts as a direct conduit for transactions. This shift presents both significant opportunities and profound challenges for the media industry.

The future of media will critically depend on the ability of media companies to navigate this commerce-driven world without losing sight of their core values and their sacred relationship with the audience. The potential for new revenue streams through content-to-commerce models could indeed revitalize media companies, providing the funds needed to produce high-quality content. However, this potential comes with the risk that media might become too closely tied to commerce, potentially undermining the quality and diversity of content.

As media becomes increasingly intertwined with commerce, ensuring that it continues to serve the needs of audiences, not just advertisers or commercial interests, will be paramount. Media companies must strive to maintain a delicate balance: leveraging new opportunities for revenue generation while steadfastly guarding the editorial independence that builds trust with their audience.

The entanglement of media with retail operations introduces complex new dynamics that affect both industries. Retailers' ability to absorb media costs into their commerce strategies and leverage first-party data for targeted advertising could shift the focus of content from audience engagement to sales promotion. Understanding these dynamics is essential for assessing the future of media and its role in society.

Forging strategic partnerships that respect and enhance media's role in society could be key. Such alliances can provide new revenue streams and innovative ways to engage audiences without compromising the integrity of media content. Collaborative efforts between legacy media companies and modern commerce giants must focus on creating synergies that benefit both parties while continuing to prioritize the audience's experience and trust.

Ultimately, the question remains: Will media in this new content-to-commerce landscape be better off? The answer is complex and multifaceted, involving careful consideration of how resources are reinvested back into media operations, how advertising strategies evolve, and how closely media companies can stay true to their mission of serving their audience.

As we move forward, the media industry must remain vigilant, ensuring that its evolution into commerce does not come at the expense of its soul. By embracing the challenges and opportunities presented by the content-to-commerce model with a clear-eyed focus on their foundational principles, media companies can not only survive but thrive, continuing to inform, inspire, and engage their audiences in meaningful ways.

10

Mourning Mass Media

Throughout this book, we've traced the evolution from the old, Newtonian Media World to today's digital landscape—a world bursting with content, brimming with new players, and dominated by powerful platforms. Change has brought many benefits: more choice, more access, and more personalization. But as with any transformation, something has been left behind.

Is this just a nostalgic lament from an author who grew up in the mass media era? Maybe. But the loss is real. The media system used to be "mass" where large, diverse audiences regularly gathered to watch, read, and listen to the same things at the same time. Today, that kind of shared experience is rare. Audience attention is fragmented across a seemingly infinite supply of content, delivered through personalized algorithms and hosted on platforms whose goals often extend well beyond media. Yes, there are still massive audiences; but they tend to congregate inside Walled Gardens, where media is increasingly a means to another end.

So what's happened to mass media? The kind that brought people together around common stories, moments, and cultural touchstones? You can still catch glimpses of it during major events like the Super Bowl or a breaking global news story. But for the most part, it's gone. And that loss matters.

Mass media wasn't just a delivery system; it was a cultural force. It shaped our shared understanding of the world and it created a foundation of stories, events, and rituals. That shared experience created a common cultural thread that shaped how we understood the world, remembered key moments, and related to one another.

This chapter explores what we've lost and why it matters. And we'll do so from the perspective of the three major players in the media economy: media companies, advertisers, and audiences. For each, the disappearance of mass media has created new challenges. And in some cases, it has exposed deep vulnerabilities that are unfolding today.

The Media Company's Dilemma: Losing Scale in a Fragmented World

In Chapter 8, we introduced the concept of scale as a key dynamic of successful business models. Scale refers to a company's ability to grow its business as efficiently and profitably as possible. In the media business, scale has always been a source of strength. And it's not just legacy media companies that want it. Every player in today's media economy—whether a streaming platform, a digital publisher, a marketer, or a creator—is chasing scale.

In media, scale comes from growing all three Cs: the amount of content a company can monetize, the number of consumers who engage with it, and the reach of its distribution channels. When a company can grow all three simultaneously, it creates a stronger, more efficient engine for monetization.

Let's break that down.

Content sits at the center of the media business. And the economics of content is uniquely favorable to scale. Once a show is produced, an article written, or a podcast recorded, the fixed cost of creation is already spent. Sharing that content with more people doesn't increase production costs. Whether one person streams a show or ten million do, the cost to produce it stays the same. Even when licensing fees or royalty payments introduce some variable costs—like paying musicians per stream or authors per download—the core logic holds: the more people who consume the content, the more revenue it can generate. That revenue can help cover fixed production costs while rewarding creators and improving profitability overall. That's the magic of scale. The content becomes more valuable the more people it reaches. And audiences benefit too: through lower prices and greater access to content that serves their wants, needs, and interests.

Channels are the infrastructure that carry content to consumers, and they come with their own complex set of fixed costs. Whether it's a broadcast network, a YouTube channel, or a proprietary streaming app, building a scalable distribution system requires significant upfront investment. These include capacity capabilities like bandwidth and server infrastructure, audience measurement systems that track performance, data management platforms that store and analyze user behavior, user experience design that optimizes content discovery and consumption, and, in many cases, licensing arrangements for third-party technologies or intellectual property. But once the infrastructure is in place, it can distribute content to ten people or ten million with relatively minor increases in cost. The more reach a company's owned or operated channels can achieve, the more efficiently they can spread content—and the more control they retain over monetization of their assets.

Consumers complete the equation. Every additional viewer, reader, or listener increases the value of both the content and the channel delivering it. But attracting and retaining consumers also carries a cost—particularly in the form of marketing and acquisition spending to bring new users into the ecosystem and customer relationship management (CRM) tools to keep them engaged over time. But the marketing investment is well worth it. Once a consumer is acquired, the marginal cost of delivering additional content is low. And the longer they stay, the greater the return from capitalizing on their payments and/or their attention. Growing the consumer base drives visibility, attracts advertisers, and strengthens network effects that can lead to even greater reach.

Scale also unlocks momentum. Network science teaches us that success often comes from connectivity: people gravitate toward what others are already consuming. The more connected an outlet becomes—whether it's a TV network, a YouTube channel, or a social feed—the more likely it is to attract additional attention. In this system, scale feeds visibility, visibility feeds engagement, and engagement feeds scale. It's a self-reinforcing cycle; the bigger you are, the easier it is to get even bigger. If you read the earlier chapter on the rise of platforms, this dynamic will sound familiar: in a networked media system, hubs with many connections naturally concentrate power. It's not a new phenomenon; it's just playing out on new infrastructure.

Back in the Newtonian Media Era, media companies had a structural advantage. With fewer content options and more limited distribution, audience attention clustered around a small number of dominant players. This made it easier to achieve scale by default, which in turn made the economics of content creation and distribution work.

Media companies no longer have that built-in advantage today. Scale still matters—but it's harder to achieve, harder to sustain, and harder to call your own. And if media companies can't achieve scale, the consequences are dire. Without the ability to amortize fixed costs across a large audience, even the most compelling content or well-designed channels may become financially unsustainable. A company that can't cover its costs can't survive. Plain and simple. The result is a shrinking pool of independent media businesses, each forced to make tough decisions about how much risk they can afford, how much ambition they can fund, and what kind of content they can realistically produce.

What happens next? The media entities left standing may not be those built to serve the public or elevate culture. Instead, we will become increasingly reliant on players for whom media is a secondary concern—a means to fuel commerce, capture attention, or support another business altogether. These companies can afford to treat media as a loss leader. But when they become the primary stewards of content and communication channels, we lose something fundamental: a vibrant, self-sustaining media ecosystem that serves the public interest. That's the real risk—not just for media companies, but for all of us.

Advertisers Trade Wasted Reach for New Complexities

The loss of scale is as profound an issue for advertisers as it is for the media companies they help to support. In the Newtonian Media Era, advertisers relied on mass media to deliver their messages to large, diverse audiences. For some, this model worked exceptionally well. Brands with broad customer bases such as consumer packaged goods (CPG) companies and quick-service restaurants (QSRs) benefited fully from mass reach. These businesses depend on selling high volumes of their products to a wide cross-section of the population. Therefore, reaching millions of people in one shot made perfect sense.

But for many other advertisers, mass media came with inefficiencies. An ad placed during a prime-time TV show might reach millions; but a significant portion of those viewers would never become customers. Marketers referred to this as "spill"—paying for audiences who didn't fit the target profile. While mass media delivered impressive scale, it lacked precision.

Then came the promise of digital media. With its rise, advertisers saw an opportunity to avoid waste by targeting only the "right" customers—those who matched detailed profiles and were more likely to engage or buy. This shift marked a move from the exposure-based models to performance-based ones introduced in the preceding chapter. Instead of judging success by how many people saw an ad; advertisers began tracking how people responded via clicks, conversions, and purchases. This direct response model became central to modern advertising logic: only pay for what works.

But while digital media allowed for more precision, it also introduced new challenges. Audience attention became scattered across countless platforms, apps, and devices. Instead of reaching many desirable customers in one place, advertisers now have to hunt them down across a fragmented digital ecosystem. And just finding them isn't enough. Thanks to the rise of Walled Gardens—platforms that control their own data and inventory—advertisers can't simply access everyone through a single marketplace. Each platform requires its own strategy, budget, creative assets, and bidding process. A campaign that once required one ad buy now demands coordination across multiple closed ecosystems.

Advertisers haven't given up on scale; they still want to reach large audiences. But now, they want to reach the right audience without paying for the wrong one. The irony is that in trying to eliminate waste, they've added layers of complexity and cost. We're left to wonder: Was the inefficiency of mass media easier to manage than the fragmentation of today? For many advertisers, it's no longer about reaching a mass audience; it's about whether they can efficiently scale the right one.

While the loss of scale creates business challenges for media companies and operational headaches for advertisers, its most profound effects may be felt by consumers. For industry players, scale is a lever of efficiency and profit. But for people like you and me, media is far more than just a delivery system. It's how we understand the world, stay connected to culture, and make sense of our place in it. When the shared rhythms of mass media break down, the impact isn't just logistical. It's personal.

Fragmented Worlds: FOMO and the Loss of Our Shared Experience

For many of you, mass media is a distant memory—if you ever knew it at all. Those who grew up in the era of media fragmentation are accustomed to personalization and niche content. In their world, a viral TikTok video with a few million views feels monumental. But for those who remember the Newtonian Media Era, when mass media truly lived up to its name, the loss is palpable. Back then, mass media was a common thread connecting entire populations, and "mass" meant tens of millions of people consuming the same content simultaneously.

Take the news, for example. In the heyday of mass media, Walter Cronkite wasn't just a news broadcaster; he was a national voice. Cronkite's broadcast created a unified understanding of the world, offering a shared reality most Americans could connect to. You didn't have to question his credibility or compare his version of events to others. You simply knew that most of the country was hearing the same story at the same time. And that alone created a powerful sense of cultural cohesion.

Today, the news landscape is fragmented beyond recognition. No single news outlet commands the same collective attention that figures like Cronkite once did. Instead, audiences choose from a wide range of news sources tailored to their preferences, politics, or values. From CNN to Fox News to Reddit threads and X (formerly Twitter), the news has splintered into countless niches, each offering its own version of reality. The result? No two people see the world in quite the same way. Where mass media once gave us a shared lens, today's fragmented news landscape offers only personalized prisms through which to view current events. For those accustomed to mass media's shared narratives, this loss of common ground is stark and unsettling.

But even those who never experienced the mass media era are feeling the effects of fragmentation. Today's audiences still crave a sense of connection to each other, to trends, and to a broader cultural conversation. Media remains a powerful cultural production system, shaping what matters and how people engage with the world. But without a central hub for shared narratives, audiences must now work harder to stay in the loop. Instead of passively receiving a curated sense of what's trending or important, people must actively chase cultural relevance across dozens of platforms.

This constant effort creates pressure—especially the fear of missing out. FOMO is real in the fragmented landscape. When no single media outlet brings the country together around major moments, audiences scramble to assemble their own cultural feeds. That often means toggling across apps, group chats, and social channels just to keep pace with what others might be watching, sharing, or discussing. It's exhausting. And it amplifies the anxiety of missing out on shared cultural moments.

While the explosion of media choice offers personalization, it also creates a burden. The gatekeepers are gone and with them, the shared media rhythms that once shaped the day. There are no longer universal cultural touchstones—no single TV show or news anchor to unite us around a common story. That doesn't mean people have stopped producing or engaging with culture. Quite the opposite. As Henry Jenkins (2006) argues in *Convergence Culture*, today's media ecosystem thrives on a feedback loop between professionally produced content and grassroots participation. The mainstream and the local feed off one another. But for that system to work well—for stories, trends, and ideas to circulate widely and gain collective meaning—there must be some infrastructure to tie it all together. Mass media once played that role. Without it, culture fragments into smaller spheres that rarely connect.

In that vacuum, the few remaining examples of mass attention, like the Super Bowl or the Academy Awards, take on outsized significance. These moments offer a rare chance to feel part of something bigger. They're nostalgic reminders of a time when media didn't just reflect culture; it helped create shared understanding across communities.

Can We Ever Go Back?

It's fair to ask: Is this just nostalgia? Would a younger author, who never knew the Newtonian Media Era, feel the same sense of loss? Maybe not in the same way. But this isn't about longing for the "good old days." It's about recognizing what mass media made possible and understanding what's been lost across the entire media ecosystem.

Media companies have lost scale. Advertisers are chasing fragmented audiences across an increasingly chaotic landscape. And audiences have lost something deeper—a shared sense of culture, identity, and collective experience.

Can we go back? Not likely. The conditions that made mass media possible have eroded. There's too much content, too much choice, and personalization has taken hold. Once audiences grow accustomed to curated feeds tailored to their individual tastes, it's nearly impossible to reassemble a single, unified stream of attention. Fragmentation isn't a phase; it's the structure now.

Yes, some version of mass will reemerge. That's how networks work. Clusters form. Hubs attract attention. But it won't be mass in the way we once knew it. It will be shaped by algorithms, commercial incentives, and platform logic—not by the shared rituals of public life.

And the questions we now face are serious ones. Can media companies survive without scale? Will advertising become so complex and fragmented that it collapses under its own weight? And if so, who will fund the next great piece of journalism, storytelling, or cultural connection?

The future of media lies in this tension. How do we rebuild a sense of collective experience in a world where mass is harder to achieve and even harder to sustain? What replaces the cultural cohesion that mass media once provided? We may not be able to put the genie back in the bottle; but we'd better start figuring out how to compensate for what we've lost. Because mass media wasn't just good for business. It was good for us.

11

Marketers Become Frenemies

The last two chapters revealed two uncomfortable truths. First, media is increasingly treated as a means to someone else's end: a tool to harvest audience attention and data, support commerce, or serve another business objective altogether. Second, the very idea of "mass" media is slipping away. With audience attention scattered across countless channels, media companies are finding it harder than ever to achieve economies of scale. And scale isn't just a nice-to-have; it's a core requirement for healthy business operations.

Now we turn to one of media's most influential partners: the marketer. In earlier chapters, we explained the concept of the dual product marketplace—where media companies serve two sets of customers: the audiences who consume content and the marketers who help fund it with advertising investments. As long as both sides saw value, the model held together.

But things have changed.

Marketers are increasingly building their own media ecosystems. They're not just pulling advertising dollars out of the system; they're pulling audiences, too. And when they do engage with media companies, they demand performance. Every dollar must prove its worth. This puts media companies in a bind—caught between shrinking ad budgets and rising expectations.

What was once a cooperative relationship has started to unravel. Friendly partners are now uneasy competitors. The alliance hasn't ended; but it has entered a new phase. Welcome to the age of frenemies.

This chapter unpacks the origins of the once codependent bond between media companies and marketers. It explores how the fundamentals of that relationship have shifted over time. Today, many media companies remain financially reliant on partners who are increasingly finding ways to bypass them altogether.

A Necessary Partnership, Never without Tension

In the Newtonian Media Era, the relationship between media companies and marketers was built on mutual necessity. Marketers had limited opportunities to reach their customers outside of paying media companies for access to their audiences. The media companies, in turn, relied on advertising dollars to cover the cost of producing content and distributing it to the public. Advertising support not only funded content creation but also kept access costs for audiences low or, in many cases, entirely free.

Yet, there was always a natural tension in this relationship. Media companies wanted to earn the greatest revenue possible for the audience attention they created, while advertisers aimed to pay the lowest price. This push and pull between maximizing revenue and minimizing costs led to constant negotiation between the two sides. Marketplace dynamics often reconciled this tension through the forces of supply and demand. Despite its imperfections, the model worked. Marketers had visibility for their advertising messages. Media companies had revenue from the sale of advertising. Audiences had efficient access to content that served their wants, needs, and interests.

In the early days of digital transformation, this dynamic continued. The internet and the plethora of websites it delivered to audiences were, for the most part, free to access. This sealed the symbiotic relationship between marketers and media companies in the early digital era. Advertising became the primary funding source for many websites. Without it, these early digital platforms would have struggled to exist. At the time, this model seemed nearly unshakeable.

But as we know, this relationship was about to face significant disruption.

What Marketers Really Need from Media

To understand the breakdown, we must first understand what marketers truly need from their relationship with media. For marketers, media is not the destination; it's a pathway. It's the mechanism that connects brands to customers across every stage of their decision-making journey.

That journey unfolds in phases. A customer might first need to become aware that a product or solution exists. Then, they might seek out more information, weigh their options, look for social proof, or hunt for the best deal. Finally, they decide whether to act. But the journey doesn't end there. Smart marketers continue to engage after the sale by reinforcing loyalty, encouraging repeat purchase, or turning customers into advocates. At each of these stages, the marketer must earn attention and deliver relevance. Media provides the access.

What marketers need, then, is a system of media that helps them deliver the right message, in the right place, and at the right time. But here's where the problem begins. Over time, the industry has adopted an artificial divide between so-called brand media and performance media. Branding efforts are treated as long-term plays, often dismissed as too soft to measure. Performance media, on the other hand, is expected to drive short-term, trackable outcomes: clicks, conversions, and sales.

This false binary has led to fractured strategies and missed opportunities. The reality is, in today's hyper-connected world, the consumer is never more than one click away from commerce. Every exposure has the potential to influence a decision, whether it's measured in brand lift or transaction data. Media doesn't live in a funnel; rather, it operates in a loop. And marketers who divide their strategies into rigid categories often lose sight of the bigger picture.

From the Customer Journey to PESO

Marketers line the pathway of the customer journey with relevant messages and experiences by using the best media tools at their disposal. And those tools don't all come from the same place. Some must be rented. Others are built. And some are earned.

That's where a powerful acronym comes in: PESO—short for Paid, Earned, Shared, and Owned media.

P.E.S.O.
The Modern Media Classification

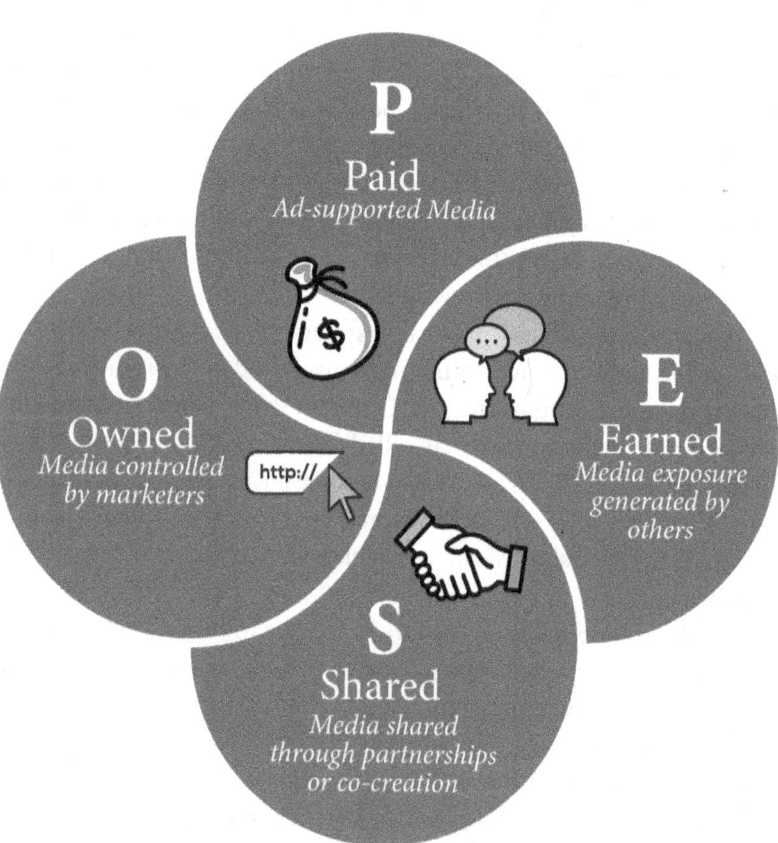

Before we move forward, let's get some important definitions out of the way (Franks 2016):

- Paid media refers to any form of media the marketer must pay to use. These are typically advertising-supported environments—TV ads, digital display ads, billboards, podcasts, and so on—where marketers pay for the right to place messages in front of an audience.
- Owned media includes all media the marketer directly controls, such as a website, mobile app, email list, or branded destinations on a social media channel.
- Earned media consists of conversations or attention a marketer earns without payment. It can take the form of press coverage, word of mouth from everyday people, or mentions from influencers—provided the endorsement wasn't paid.
- Shared media is when two marketers agree to share their owned media assets with each other for mutual benefit. This is not to be confused with "sharing" in the general sense of users reposting or amplifying content across digital platforms. Thanks to open circuits, sharing happens everywhere. Shared media, in the PESO framework, is more intentional and collaborative.

At a glance, PESO seems like a helpful way to think about media strategy. But there's more to the story. Each quadrant of PESO carries a different financial weight, and that creates a powerful bias.

Let's start with paid media. Even though advertising can build brand equity, drive sales in both the short and long term, and support customer lifetime value, financial accounting doesn't treat it as an investment. Instead, paid media is classified as a current expense—recorded in full as soon as the ad runs.

In contrast, owned and shared media often receive more favorable treatment. Owned media assets like websites and mobile apps can be considered intangible brand assets that retain residual value. And earned media—when it's positive—is essentially free. It comes with no direct cost, no financial penalty, and substantial upside. It's the icing on the cake.

And so, we arrive at the marketer's modern-day riddle:

Pay as little as you can, own as much of the brand experience as possible, and earn favorable brand mentions in a socially networked world (Franks 2016).

It's eloquent. It's logical. And it's unsolvable.

Marketers are under pressure to reduce paid media expenses, shift as much of the customer journey as possible to their owned environments, and hope for earned media to extend their reach. The PESO model isn't just a media planning framework. It's a reflection of how financial incentives and structural bias are reshaping the media ecosystem—often to the detriment of media companies who depend on paid media to survive.

The Rise of Owned Media in Modern Marketing

Once marketers internalized the idea that paid media was an expense to be minimized, the natural next step was clear: take ownership of the customer journey. Why pay a third party to rent access to an audience when you can build the channel yourself?

This mindset has sparked one of the most profound shifts in modern marketing: the rise of owned media as a central marketing asset. Marketers are no longer just placing messages within someone else's content; they're producing and distributing content of their own. Instead of relying solely on media companies to reach their audiences, marketers are building their own digital environments—websites, mobile apps, social pages, email newsletters, content hubs, and even full-scale media operations that rival traditional publishers.

Examples of early pioneers illustrate how the definition of media ownership has expanded. Long before digital content hubs and branded podcasts, P&G helped invent the concept of brand-owned media by creating the soap opera. The company literally produced daytime dramas as a platform to promote its household brands. Decades later, Red Bull reimagined what a beverage brand could be by building a robust media empire that includes live events, documentaries, and its own film production unit. Glossier emerged as a content-first beauty brand rooted in social media and community engagement. General Electric was among the first to experiment with branded podcasts, launching *The Message* in 2015—an eight-part sci-fi series that blurred the lines between storytelling and brand narrative. LEGO built entire worlds of owned entertainment through films, video games, magazines, and digital channel assets across nearly every available channel. And brands like Nike and Peloton redefined what it means to control a content environment by integrating media directly into their products and services.

Today, what was once pioneering is now the price of entry. Nearly every marketer has some form of owned media—whether it's a website, YouTube channel, podcast, mobile app, or social content hub. It's no longer a bold experiment. It's expected.

For marketers, the appeal is clear. Owned media offers control: control over the message, the environment, the user experience, and, most importantly, the audience data. The more of the customer journey they own, the less reliant they are on external platforms. And the more they control, the more they can tailor the experience to meet their specific goals.

But here's the catch: to the audience, it's all just media. Whether a message comes from a marketer or from a traditional media company, people judge it the same way. Is it interesting? Is it useful? Is it worth my time? If marketers want to play the role of media owners, they must also adopt the responsibilities of publishers—creating content that serves the wants, needs, and interests of their audience. Owned media isn't a free pass to promote endlessly. It's a commitment to deliver value.

And getting audiences to engage with that content is no small feat. With so much clutter in the content marketplace, even the best branded websites, YouTube series, or thought-leadership hubs rarely get discovered on their own. Paid social boosts, search ads, native placements, and even traditional advertisements are often required to bring traffic to these owned environments. Ironically, marketers still find themselves paying ad-supported media companies—not to sell their products and services directly but to promote their owned channels. In trying to avoid the cost of paid media, they end up paying for it anyway—just with a different objective.

Still, if they do it well, the payoff is clear: marketers become less dependent on paid media altogether. They reduce their advertising spend—the very dollars that once helped sustain the media ecosystem. And to make matters worse for media companies, owned media doesn't just pull dollars. It pulls audience attention. The more time people spend engaging with brand-owned content, the less time—and value—remains for traditional media players.

It's a double hit: less revenue and less attention.

The Precision Trap: What's Left for Paid Media?

Owned media may reduce a brand's reliance on paid advertising, but it doesn't eliminate the need for it altogether. Marketers still need to reach audiences beyond their owned platforms—whether they're looking to attract new prospects or reconnect with existing customers during key moments in their journey. As a result, paid media continues to play an important role.

But today, it carries more pressure than ever to deliver results. Advertising isn't just expected to reach people—it's expected to do so precisely and deliver measurable outcomes.

We used to accept that advertising came with some waste. John Wanamaker, the nineteenth-century department store pioneer, famously quipped, "Half the money I spend on advertising is wasted; the trouble is, I don't know which half." For decades, that quote served as both a lament and a shrug—an acknowledgment of advertising's inherent inefficiencies. But today, marketers are expected to do something about it.

This shift has fundamentally changed expectations. In the past, advertisers accepted that some audience "spill"—reaching people outside their core target—was inevitable. Today, the landscape has changed. Technology now allows advertisers to target with precision and pay only for performance. For marketers, this is an efficient solution. But for media companies, it undermines the economies of scale that once allowed them to thrive.

As marketers have grown more sophisticated in their ability to track, measure, and analyze customer data, their focus has narrowed to highly specific audience segments—those most likely to convert into immediate sales or desired actions. This precision targeting can be incredibly efficient in the short term. But it also has significant drawbacks.

By focusing almost exclusively on these "desirable" audiences, marketers disregard the broader value of reaching diverse or less easily measured segments. Media companies, which once offered the opportunity to engage with wide-ranging audiences, now find themselves challenged to deliver on marketers' hyper-focused demands.

Has Attribution Gone Too Far?

With the rise of performance-based advertising, where payment is tied directly to measurable outcomes like clicks or sales, a critical question emerges: Is it fair to hold media companies accountable for product sales?

There's a lot that happens between a consumer seeing an ad and making a purchase. From researching the product to comparing prices or even deciding that now isn't the right time to buy, there are countless steps in the consumer journey that fall outside of the media company's control. Yet, under these performance-driven models, media companies are only paid on the back end—once a sale or measurable action is completed.

It raises a deeper question: Where do we draw the line between the responsibility of the media company and the responsibility of the marketer? If an ad doesn't immediately translate to sales, is it solely the media company's fault? What about the quality of the product, the timing of the campaign, or the competitive landscape? These are all factors the media company has no say in.

Of course, some media companies say, "bring it on." They're confident in their ability to deliver. But for many, this model undervalues the broader role that media plays in supporting advertisers' brands. Media isn't just about driving immediate conversions; it's about building long-term brand awareness, influencing perceptions, and creating cultural relevance.

A Strained Relationship, Exposed

Marketers haven't abandoned media companies entirely, but the relationship has undeniably changed. By building robust owned ecosystems, they've reduced their reliance on ad-supported media. In doing so, they've redirected both attention and revenue. Every minute a consumer spends engaging with a marketer's content is a minute not spent with a media company. That's a double hit: fewer advertising dollars flowing into traditional media and less audience attention to monetize.

To make matters more complicated, when marketers do turn to paid media, they expect more from it than ever before. Precision targeting. Attribution. Proof of performance. Media companies that once thrived by delivering mass audiences now face pressure to deliver only the "right" audience—and to prove that they've delivered measurable business outcomes.

It's not a clean break. It's a strained relationship. Media companies and marketers still need each other. But the balance of power has shifted. Marketers have new tools, new options, and new expectations. And media companies are left to reckon with the consequences.

Can This Relationship Be Repaired?

Marketers and media companies are no longer in sync—but they're not fully apart, either. The codependent relationship that once sustained the media ecosystem is fraying. Marketers have built their own media machines, diverted attention, demanded more accountability, and spent less. Media companies, meanwhile, are left scrambling to reinvent their models in a world where they have less control over audience access and advertiser expectations.

Yet, for all the strain, the need for collaboration hasn't gone away. Owned media may be powerful, but it's resource-intensive and hard to scale. Precision marketing may be efficient, but it risks narrowing any brand's reach and cultural relevance. And even performance-focused campaigns need context, storytelling, and emotional resonance—the very assets media companies are built to deliver.

This moment calls for more than just negotiation. It demands a strategic rebalancing. Can marketers evolve beyond short-termism and recommit to the value of independent media? Can media companies find new ways to prove their worth without becoming commoditized intermediaries?

The relationship is strained—but not yet severed.

Can this relationship be saved? Or are media companies and marketers destined to remain frenemies that compete for attention in an increasingly fragmented world? Only time will tell. But one thing is clear: the days of easy cooperation between marketers and media companies are over.

12

Marketplace Complexity

In the prior chapter, we explored how the relationship between media companies and marketers has shifted into one best described as "frenemies." Despite the tension, these two players remain economically intertwined. As long as ad-supported media exists and marketers continue investing in advertising, the two will remain economically dependent on each other—even if the alliance is uneasy.

But if strained relationships weren't enough, the modern marketplaces that connect these two parties have become a tangled web. We can't discuss the chaos of the media business without confronting the convoluted systems used to buy and sell advertising. Historically, these marketplaces were relatively straightforward. Not anymore.

The rise of programmatic marketplaces has delivered unprecedented precision, speed, and scale to digital advertising campaigns. But these gains come at a cost. Complexity bias now dominates the prevailing wisdom.

So what is complexity bias? It's a term widely used in popular psychology and behavioral science to describe our tendency to overvalue intricate systems. It reflects the belief that more complexity must mean more intelligence, more sophistication, or more value.

Digital advertising marketplaces have become so complex that attempting to explain them in a book designed to bring clarity is nearly impossible. And yet, we tolerate and even celebrate the complexity.

Perhaps because we believe anything so elaborate must be brilliant. But maybe it's not.

Marc Pritchard, CBO (chief brand officer) at P&G, sounded the alarm at the IAB (Interactive Advertising Bureau) Annual Leadership Meeting all the way back in 2017. In his now-famous speech, he described the digital advertising supply chain as "murky at best and fraudulent at worst," citing the lack of transparency, inconsistent metrics, and hidden agency fees. He demanded reforms: standardized viewability metrics, third-party accredited measurement, and full transparency (Pritchard 2017).

Yet here we are, years later, and the system remains as convoluted as ever. Complexity bias still props up a marketplace that favors intermediaries rather than the marketers trying to reach audiences or the media companies trying to serve them. The real winners in today's convoluted marketplace are those who profit from the confusion. The lack of transparency, the dense web of intermediaries, and the multilayered infrastructure all serve to enrich players on both the supply and demand sides of the marketplace.

How bad is it? At the end of 2023, *Adweek* reported an ANA study on programmatic transparency that identified only one-third of programmatic advertising dollars making it to the end user (Perloff 2023). Stop and ponder this for a moment. We've built a marketplace ecosystem with a 67 percent overhead rate. That's just crazy.

From Handshakes to Automation

Not long ago, advertising deals were made between real people. Buyers and sellers negotiated over lunch, on the phone, by fax (remember fax machines?), or by email. These "handshake deals" were built on relationships, trust, and experience. Sure, each side wondered if they could have gotten a better deal. Marketers questioned whether they'd overpaid, and media companies hoped they hadn't undersold. But the system worked well enough, especially when the choices were limited and familiar.

Back then, the supply of advertising opportunities was manageable. You could track available time and space across TV, newspapers, magazines, radio, billboards, and websites using nothing more than a spreadsheet. As long as media options stayed within human reach, people could handle the process.

Then everything changed.

As digital media grew, advertising capacity swelled beyond anything we had seen and managed before. New websites launched by the second. And with it came new capacity to fuel the early vestiges of digital advertising. Suddenly, there were too many options for any team of humans to sort through. The supply had outgrown our ability to manage it.

At the same time, the question of price still loomed. Marketers still didn't know if they were paying too much. Media companies still didn't know if they were leaving money on the table. A new system was needed—one that could handle the massive number of digital advertising opportunities and take the guesswork out of pricing.

This is where Google stepped in.

Google didn't invent auctions, but it made them a mainstream way of buying and selling digital advertising. Through its AdWords platform, Google created a system where advertisers could say how much they were willing to pay to place an ad. The highest bidder would win the opportunity but only pay the price of the second-highest bidder, plus a small amount. This kind of auction helped everyone see the real market value of an ad opportunity. It gave marketers more control over what they were willing to spend, and it removed the mystery around what something should cost.

Google's system also did something else: it showed that every single advertising opportunity—every search, every website visit, every video view—could become its own mini marketplace. Instead of one big deal covering a block of time or space, each advertising occasion was decided on its own and in real time. The system could make decisions instantly and at scale; something humans simply couldn't do.

To make this work, Google didn't just launch auctions; they built the tools to support them. Marketers got access to bidding platforms that helped automate their decisions. Publishers (media companies) connected their ad spaces to Google so they could sell available advertising inventory in real time. It was fast, automatic, and efficient. And it worked reasonably well.

At first, this approach was used mostly for keyword search advertising and website banner advertising (known as digital display advertising).

Traditional advertising-supported media still relied on human negotiation and fixed schedules. But Google had lit a spark.

Google proved that advertising marketplaces could be faster, smarter, and more dynamic. And once the industry saw what was possible, the auction marketplace started spreading. This laid the foundation for what would soon grow into the programmatic marketplace we know today.

Programmatic Explained

When Google introduced digital ad auctions, it gave marketers a way to buy advertising in real time, based on the value of an audience impression at that moment. Programmatic advertising took that same idea and made it personal. It added the ability to target individuals based on who they were, not just where they were.

This marked a fundamental shift in how advertising was bought and sold. In the early days of digital, advertisers placed ads based on content. If you sold running shoes, you might bid on certain keywords or choose to advertise on a sports blog. If you sold baby formula, you'd look for relevant search terms and place display ads on parenting websites. The logic was contextual: place your message where relevant content lived.

Programmatic expanded that logic. In addition to targeting the content, it offered the opportunity to target the person wherever they happened to be in the programmatic ecosystem. Suddenly, it didn't matter if the right consumer was on a news site, a game, or a weather app. If their data signaled that they were a valuable audience, a marketer could reach them instantly.

To make this work, the advertising ecosystem had to build a new kind of infrastructure that was fast, automated, and fueled by a lot of audience data. Programmatic became the system that connected marketers to individual advertising opportunities in real time. But it also introduced a new cast of intermediaries to make that system function. On the buy side, Demand-Side Platforms (DSPs) helped marketers decide when to bid, how much to spend, and which ad to show. On the sell side, Supply-Side Platforms (SSPs) enabled media companies to manage and monetize their available ad space. And sitting in the middle were ad exchanges, the digital marketplaces where buyers and sellers came together.

The Programmatic Ecosystem
A Market Where Buyers and Sellers Exchange Value

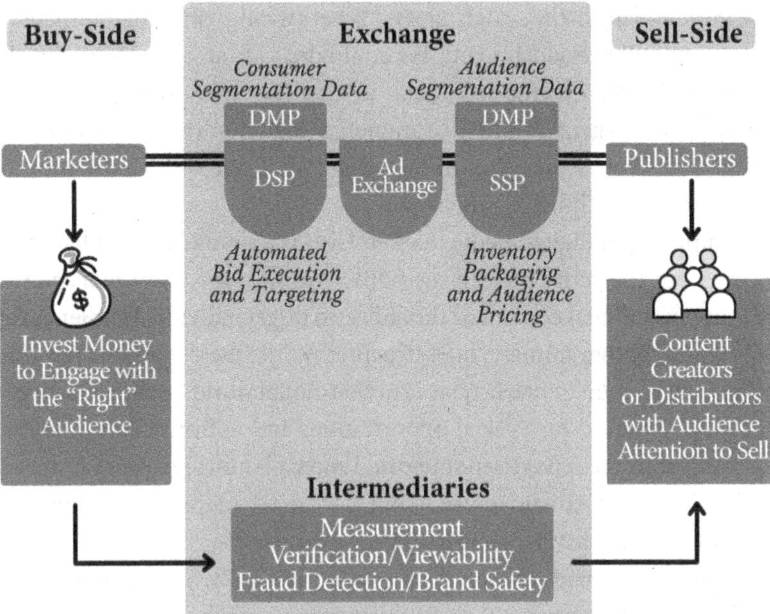

This infrastructure allowed programmatic to scale rapidly beyond the open web. Soon it was powering ad delivery across mobile apps, connected TV, audio platforms, digital out-of-home screens, and even video games. In each case, marketers used real-time data to bid for audience attention, and the winning ad was slotted in dynamically.

At its best, programmatic offered precision, efficiency, and automation. It turned advertising into a data-driven, real-time engine—one that could theoretically reach the right person, with the right message, at the right moment, and across any digital environment.

But all of this came with a trade-off: complexity.

What began as a streamlined solution quickly grew into an elaborate system with dozens of moving parts, powered by data feeds, algorithms, and a growing network of intermediaries to make each part of the value chain work. Each promised to optimize some piece of the process. But together, they created a tangled web of transactions, costs, and questions.

Which brings us to the next chapter in this story: What went wrong?

The Complexity Problem

Take a break from reading for a moment and go into your web browser and type the following in the search query: "What's wrong with programmatic?" The results will overwhelm you! We could dedicate an entire book (likely volumes of books) trying to explain all that has gone wrong with what started as an elegant solution to monetize digital advertising inventory and give marketers precision in targeting. We're left with a labyrinthine system that is anything but efficient.

Complexity in digital media marketplaces is a significant problem. Yet, we can't put the genie back in the bottle. We simply cannot manage the vast supply of digital content or the ability to target individual audiences at scale without programmatic infrastructure. While there may still be a role for human-to-human marketplaces in this digital world, it's now relatively small and reserved for special opportunities and upfront commitments. For the rest of the advertiser-supported media landscape, programmatic remains the only realistic solution. But if we don't address the complexity embedded in these systems, we're heading for trouble.

Einstein once said, "If you can't explain it simply, you don't know it well enough" (Calaprice 2011). In this instance, maybe there's no simple explanation because what we have on our hands is a hot mess.

Too Many Exchanges, No Big Picture

At the heart of the problem is the overabundance of exchanges themselves. Both buyers and sellers have to determine which exchanges to use to do their business. What's the problem with choice? Isn't competition a good thing? In many instances, yes. But in some instances, we need consolidation in order to deliver essential services much like other utilities. If we consider that the infrastructure that facilitates the exchange between marketers and media companies is an essential service, we need consolidation and oversight. Ironically, despite all the different exchanges in the programmatic ecosystem today, we still are facing a significant divide that is referred to as: the open web versus the Walled Gardens. The tech giants operate entirely within their own worlds, requiring marketers to buy directly through their proprietary systems. No one has a clear line of sight on an audience as they travel across the digital media realm. Audience impressions are tightly bound to their respective domains, and no one can see the big picture anymore.

Buyer Beware

The programmatic marketplace, especially the open marketplaces, creates opportunities for digital media of all kinds to earn revenue off their wares. But, as we discussed earlier in the book, not all content is created equal. Content ranges from high quality all the way to clickbait. Yet there's no standard rating system for the quality of inventory in the marketplace. In order to address this cornucopia of "stuff" that lands in the same open marketplaces, the system has evolved into different auction marketplaces. Private Marketplaces (PMPs) have emerged as a solution to the wide range of content offerings and the concerns around content quality and brand safety. In a PMP, publishers invite a select group of marketers to bid on premium inventory. But this comes with its own challenges: higher costs, limited reach, and still more fragmentation. Meanwhile, programmatic direct allows marketers to bypass auctions altogether and purchase inventory directly from publishers at a fixed price. While this provides more control, it further muddies the waters by introducing another layer of transaction complexity.

At the end of the day, both marketers and media companies need a way to determine the quality standards of the content that attracts audiences in the auction marketplace. Without a system of ratings and standards, the marketplace is trying to resolve the issue with more layers and even more exchanges to manage.

A Full-Time Business

Programmatic advertising has become so complex that it now requires its own dedicated teams, technology infrastructure, audience data, and expertise to manage effectively. Marketers can no longer rely solely on general media buyers to handle this intricate ecosystem. Instead, they must hire specialists and/or build in-house capabilities in order to participate in the marketplace. While we're used to talking about efficiencies (or lack thereof) in media pricing itself, we now need to look at efficiency in terms of the operational costs incurred to buy digital advertising in the programmatic marketplace. What used to be a relatively small team of media buyers has now become an army of programmatic operators to run this engine.

On the media company side, programmatic has created an entirely new layer of resource demands. Publishers need to build or acquire ad tech infrastructures to manage their digital inventory effectively. Beyond technology, media companies also require a dedicated workforce of programmatic specialists who can manage relationships with the advertising exchanges, monitor inventory pricing, and ensure that ads meet quality standards. As a result, programmatic advertising has transformed from a facilitation mechanism into an intricate ecosystem, swelled by the sheer volume of players, platforms, and strategies required to make it work.

In effect, programmatic has grown into its own economy. It's no longer a simple tool but a business model that demands constant attention, investment, and innovation. Both marketers and media companies must invest heavily in human capital and technology to remain competitive. It's shifting the industry's focus from merely buying and selling advertising space and time to managing the complexities of automated, data-driven transactions at scale.

Some critics argue that today's programmatic platforms can be managed by small, lean teams. After all, the algorithms do the heavy lifting. But that assumes full trust in black-box systems. When you surrender control to automation, you also risk losing sight of how decisions are made and who benefits from them. That's precisely why an ecosystem of specialists has emerged. These experts aren't just pushing buttons; they're working behind the scenes to ensure ads are placed in the right environments, traffic is legitimate, performance is tracked, and reporting makes sense to the broader organization.

So yes, the headcount may be smaller in some cases but only if you hand over the reins entirely to the machines. In reality, programmatic has become so complex that it has spawned an entire industry to support it. What was once a handshake deal between buyer and seller now requires armies not just of people, but of platforms, protocols, and partners to manage the chaos we've created.

Are the Ads Even Real?

One of the most uncomfortable truths about programmatic advertising is that not every ad impression is equal or even real. As marketers chase precision and performance, they must also ask two simple but critical questions: Was the ad actually seen? And was the viewer even human?

Let's start with viewability. In programmatic marketplaces, an ad is counted as "served" the moment it's delivered to a webpage or app. But that doesn't mean a human ever saw it. The ad might have loaded at the bottom of a page no one scrolled to or appeared for just a fraction of a second before the user clicked away. Industry standards now attempt to define viewability such as requiring 50 percent of pixels to be in view for at least one or two seconds (depending upon the type of ad). But even those benchmarks don't guarantee meaningful exposure. For marketers trying to connect with real people and measure real outcomes, the idea that their advertising budgets may be spent on unseen impressions is deeply troubling.

But viewability is just the beginning. The more disturbing issue is fraudulent traffic. These are impressions generated not by people but by bots. Fraudsters have become increasingly sophisticated, using automated systems to mimic human behavior, inflate site traffic, and trigger ad views that never had a chance to make an impact. These bots can "watch" videos, "click" ads, and even "navigate" websites, all while marketers pay as though genuine engagement occurred.

Estimates vary, but industry audits routinely suggest that billions of advertising dollars are wasted each year on non-human traffic. And because programmatic systems operate at speed and scale, detecting and eliminating fraud isn't easy. It requires continuous investment in verification tools, independent audits, and robust partnerships with measurement providers. Even then, fraudsters often stay one step ahead.

In the end, the complexity and automation that make programmatic efficient also create openings for abuse. Without trust in the integrity of the advertising exposure itself, all the benefits of real-time bidding and data-driven targeting start to unravel. Marketers don't just want reach; they want verified, viewable human attention.

Will Programmatic Crash before We Fix It?

The parallels between the stock market and the programmatic advertising marketplace are striking. Both systems rely on the seamless exchange of value between buyers and sellers, and both involve complex layers of intermediaries that facilitate automated transactions. However, the stock market has something that the programmatic marketplace lacks—a long history of regulation and oversight.

Stock markets offer a structured environment with only two major exchanges in the United States, NYSE (New York Stock Exchange) and NASDAQ (National Association of Securities Dealers Automated Quotations), which centralizes transactions and simplifies trading. They are regulated by the Securities and Exchange Commission (known as the SEC), which ensures oversight and enforces rules that protect participants and maintain market integrity. Stocks are evaluated for their quality in order to provide investors with clear information about what they're buying. Additionally, stock exchanges have transparency in fees to allow traders to see exactly what they're paying to intermediaries. Applying these principles to the programmatic marketplace could bring much-needed transparency, efficiency, and trust.

And that regulation didn't come easily; it was forged in the aftermath of catastrophic market failures that shook the economy to its core. The 1929 stock market crash led to the Great Depression, which devastated economies and livelihoods worldwide. It was this collapse that forced the creation of regulatory bodies like the SEC, along with strict rules to prevent another financial disaster. In 1987, the stock market saw another sudden collapse, known as Black Monday, which spurred further reforms in trading and risk management. Both events showed that regulation follows catastrophe.

What if we could prevent such a crash from happening in the programmatic advertising marketplace? The digital advertising ecosystem, though lucrative, is also vulnerable. The sheer complexity of the supply chain, the lack of transparency, and the inefficiencies created by too many intermediaries siphoning off value could lead to a major disruption. Rather than waiting for a crisis to force regulation and accountability, we should take action now. But regulation alone won't fix the deeper problem. We need to ask a more fundamental question about what kind of media system we're building and who it's ultimately meant to serve.

Programmatic versus the 3Cs

It's one thing for the programmatic marketplace to be inefficient, fragmented, or even vulnerable to fraud. But perhaps the more profound issue is this: Who was programmatic really built for? At its core, the entire system privileges the marketer's needs by allowing them to isolate the consumer, buy attention one impression at a time, and drive down cost wherever possible. The media company's content, once the primary source of value, is reduced to a targeting surface. The channel? Just a pipe.

That logic flies in the face of the 3Cs relationship that has served as a guiding principle throughout this book: media only works when Consumers, Content, and Channels are in balance. Audiences consume content that is relevant, engaging, and trustworthy. Channels deliver that content in ways that are accessible and intuitive. The marketer, in a healthy media system, is a guest. They should be welcomed only when their advertising message enhances or funds the experience in a way that respects this delicate relationship.

Programmatic flipped that relationship. It treats content as interchangeable. Channels as utilities. And consumers as data profiles to be mined. It asks: How cheaply can I buy this person's attention right now? That's not just a technical flaw; it's an existential one.

There are encouraging signs. The industry is showing renewed interest in contextual advertising, which restores value to content environments and recognizes that where an advertisement appears still matters. But that shift is reactive. It doesn't erase the fact that we've built an infrastructure that commodifies attention and strips value from the very entities—media companies and their content—that made audience attention possible in the first place.

It doesn't have to be this way. Auctions can elevate. Think of Sotheby's, where scarcity, story, and setting create markets that honor the value of what's being sold. But in programmatic, the auction hasn't elevated media; it has cheapened it. And unless we reckon with that, we may find ourselves with a marketplace optimized for everything but the one sacred relationship that matters most: the relationship between Content, Consumers, and Channels. Everything else is secondary.

13

How Well Is the Media Business Serving Its Customers?

Throughout Part II, we have uncovered how the business side of media has returned us to chaos. We examined the fundamentals of the media business, the dynamics of effective business models, and how media marketplaces trade value between buyers and sellers. We explored how these fundamentals have been strained by varying business motives, the loss of scale, marketers' shifting priorities, and the increasing complexity of the media marketplaces themselves.

But before we move on, there's one vital question left to ask: How well is the media business serving its most important customer? Somewhere along the way, we've lost sight of the answer. At the end of the day, the only customer who truly matters is the audience—the person who shows up to consume content through a channel. If we fail to keep this primary customer engaged and satisfied, then none of the ancillary interests will hold. And yet, the audience's needs are too often treated as secondary to short-term revenue goals, advertiser demands, or platform control.

This isn't a new problem. It's plagued the media business since the dawn of advertiser-supported economic models. And as those models continue to proliferate, we must question whether media companies are straying even further from their primary mission. Because without the audience's attention, there are no other masters to serve.

And so, the most pressing question remains: How well is the current state of media serving its only true customer? To answer this burning question, we need to evaluate how well the media business model functions from the audience's point of view. That's what this chapter aims to explore.

A Customer-Centric Lens: SIVA

Before we go any further, let's clarify what it means to be truly customer-centric. It's important to understand that traditional business models were built from the inside out. In the classic 4P's marketing model, companies focused on what they wanted to sell (Product), how much they could charge (Price), how they would persuade customers to buy (Promotion), and where consumers could buy these products and services (Place). While the 4P's framework served many organizations well in a supply-constrained world, it fails to fully account for the empowered consumer in today's attention economy.

That's why Professor Don Schultz, the father of Integrated Marketing Communications, proposed a reframing. Instead of thinking about what you're trying to sell, start by thinking about what your customers need. This shift from inside-out (company-centered) to outside-in (customer-centered) thinking is what Schultz framed as the SIVA model: Solution, Information, Value, and Access (Dev and Schultz 2005).

SIVA mirrors the 4Ps, with each component reframed to emphasize the consumer's point of view.

- Solution replaces Product. Instead of asking "What am I selling?," ask "What problem am I solving for the consumer?"
- Information replaces Promotion. Instead of pushing a message, help the consumer make informed decisions through relevant, timely information from trustworthy sources.
- Value replaces Price. It's the sum of the benefits both the consumer and the company receive from the relationship. It's a win-win for both parties.
- Access replaces Place. It's not about where you put your products; it's about ensuring that the consumer can engage with your offering however and whenever they choose.

This framework requires companies—media companies included—to see the business through the eyes of their customers. And that's precisely what this chapter will do. We will use SIVA to evaluate how well the media ecosystem is delivering on the needs of its most essential customer: the audience.

How Well Is Media Delivering on SIVA?

While today's digital media landscape offers unprecedented choice and convenience, it also presents new challenges from the audience's perspective. Evaluating the media business through the lens of SIVA reveals both signs of progress and pressure points. The very abundance that defines the ecosystem—more content, more platforms, more personalized experiences—can also become a source of strain. Too much content, too many ads, too many subscriptions, and increasingly complex uses of audience data are beginning to test the limits of what consumers are willing to manage. These tensions span all four dimensions of SIVA and raise an essential question: Is the media ecosystem truly delivering on its promise to the consumer? After all, the sacred 3Cs relationship depends on media offering conveniently accessible content that serves the wants, needs, and interests of the audience—the consumer in the 3Cs equation.

Solution: When More Becomes Too Much

Content is the ultimate solution in the relationship between media companies and their audience. It informs, entertains, inspires, and connects. At its best, content helps people fulfill needs, express identities, and stay in sync with their communities. And thanks to digital media, there's more of it than ever before.

But more isn't always better. The explosion of content that's coming from media companies, marketers, influencers, retailers, platforms, and everyday users has made the simple act of choosing what to consume a daily challenge. The question is no longer just what to watch, read, or listen to—but who created it, why it was made, where to find it, and whether it's worth your time. Navigating this mix requires time, discernment, and access—placing a growing burden on the consumer. What was once a streamlined media relationship now feels like a full-time job. The very thing meant to serve the audience is starting to overwhelm it.

Information: Who Do You Trust?

In a world overwhelmed by content, audiences don't just need more options; they need help making sense of them. That's the role of information in the SIVA model: providing guidance that enables informed decisions. In the Newtonian Media Era, that guidance mainly came from professional gatekeepers. Programming directors decided which shows to put on a television network (and on what day and time). Editors decided what content was worthy of being published in the pages of newspapers and magazines. Radio stations curated playlists and, at times, they empowered their disc jockeys to add songs to the mix. And, there were culture critics who commented on all this fare. And we had program guides to help audiences navigate choices across the landscape. Today, we still have professional curators; but they're just one voice in a crowded mix of influencers, algorithms, and branded content.

Recommendation systems now guide most content choices in today's digital realm. However, they are designed to maximize engagement within a single platform, rather than help audiences explore their options across the ecosystem. These systems are powered by personal data and opaque algorithms, raising real questions about privacy, transparency, and bias. Are they serving the audience or the platform's business goals?

Audiences need trustworthy, objective information to evaluate how best to spend their valuable time. But in today's environment, trust is splintered. Critics, creators, and machines all compete to shape what's seen, heard, and shared. The result? A landscape where it's harder to know what content deserves attention—and who gets to decide.

Value: A Shifting Exchange

In the traditional media relationship, value was clear: audiences gained access to content in exchange for their time, attention, or money. Whether it was a subscription fee, ad exposure, or both, the content itself was the center of the deal and it was easy to see what was being given and received.

But as business models have evolved, content is no longer always the primary object of value. In some cases, the exchange is now powered by audience data that is collected passively and monetized in ways the audience may not fully realize. In other cases, content is simply a vehicle to drive commerce, with value measured not by what the audience consumes but by what they buy.

The question is whether content still carries intrinsic value or if it's just a means to something else. As the value equation drifts away from the content–audience relationship, it becomes harder to know what, exactly, is being valued—and by whom.

Access: Good Luck Finding Everything

In today's digital world, audiences expect to access media on their terms— streaming on demand, watching across devices, and consuming content whenever and wherever it suits them. On the surface, access seems more open than ever. But in practice, getting to the right content often requires navigating a fragmented, paywalled, and ad-saturated ecosystem.

According to Yahoo Finance, the average consumer now spends nearly $1,000 per year on media subscriptions (Safane 2024). And despite that investment, access still comes with trade-offs: escalating ad loads, fragmented content libraries, and too many services to manage. Even in instances where media is free to access and supported with advertising, the volume of commercial interruptions can make free access feel like anything but.

The result? Fatigue. Subscription fatigue. Advertising fatigue. Decision fatigue. When it becomes too hard or too expensive to complete a media diet, audiences pull back (Malthouse et al. 2024). And when access becomes a burden, the overall value of the media experience starts to erode.

SIVA Exposes Flaws

In sum, the media ecosystem is more advanced, more dynamic, and more data-driven than ever before. And yet, from the audience's point of view, that progress comes with a price. While media companies may claim to deliver the right Solutions, offer trustworthy Information, create mutual Value, and enable flexible Access, the reality is more complicated.

Audiences now shoulder much of the burden once managed by media companies—filtering content, navigating fragmented platforms, evaluating tradeoffs, and deciding what's truly worth their time, money, or data. The result is a system that often feels more extractive than reciprocal.

Short-Term Thinking, Long-Term Consequences

If media companies want to address all the shortfalls that the SIVA model illustrates, they will need to recommit to customer centricity—not just in language, but in practice. SIVA exposed a host of problems that need to be addressed. Yet, these are just the tip of the iceberg. Underneath all the challenges outlined by SIVA is a deeper issue: the media industry's obsession with short-term outcomes.

Short-termism isn't new. The media business has long operated under immediate revenue pressures. In the Newtonian Media Era, this often meant maximizing audience size to sell the next ad. Today, it's evolved into something more insidious. With digital metrics offering real-time feedback, every impression, click, or conversion is scrutinized. Business performance is measured not in years or quarters, but in days or even hours.

This mindset is particularly visible in the advertising world, where marketers increasingly focus on immediate performance: Did the ad generate a sale? Did the content convert? If not, move on. Audiences are no longer valued for their potential; they're judged only by their momentary behavior. This transactional approach turns audiences into disposable assets rather than long-term customers.

Media companies often find themselves trapped in the same cycle. Those backed by private equity or venture capital are under immense pressure to grow fast or prove traction immediately. And for publicly traded media companies, the pressure of quarterly earnings can be relentless. These businesses don't have the luxury of a long-term runway. They need wins now. And that urgency distorts decision-making. Instead of investing in audience loyalty and sustainable models, they optimize for speed, surface metrics, and quick returns.

The irony is that advertisers, media companies, and content–commerce players alike all depend on audiences—but only when it suits their timeline. If a user isn't ready to buy today, they're invisible. If an article doesn't perform immediately, it gets buried. If a new program doesn't spike engagement within a few episodes, it's pulled. Meanwhile, the long-term value of building a relationship with the audience by gaining their trust, earning their loyalty is left unrealized.

This short-term orientation stands in stark contrast to the principles of customer centricity and the SIVA framework we explored earlier. It's not enough to deliver a onetime value. The media business must think about audience relationships in terms of duration and depth, not just immediacy and reach.

Customer Lifetime Value: A Long-Term Play in a Short-Term World

That's where Customer Lifetime Value (CLV) comes in. It may be one of the most underleveraged assets in the media business today. While marketers in subscription and loyalty-based industries have long relied on CLV to drive long-term growth, it remains a largely untapped metric in media models that chase attention in the moment.

CLV is a foundational concept: it estimates the net profit a company can expect to earn from a customer over the entire span of the relationship. It's typically calculated by multiplying average revenue per customer by average customer lifespan and subtracting the costs to acquire and serve them. In simple terms: How valuable is this relationship over time?

But CLV is more than a formula; it's a mindset. It reframes the customer not as a transaction, but as a relationship worth cultivating. The longer you keep that relationship, the more valuable it becomes. And in a media ecosystem where attention is scarce and fleeting, loyal audiences are more than a nice-to-have; they're a strategic advantage.

Audience loyalty gives you leverage. It increases the odds that your audience will still be there when other players—advertisers, commerce platforms, and distribution partners—want to connect with them. That's why investing in loyalty today is a hedge against the volatility of tomorrow. It's more cost-effective to retain an existing customer than to acquire a new one.

But there's even more at stake in media. Thanks to the networked nature of today's digital ecosystem, audiences aren't just consumers, they're connectors. When someone is deeply engaged with your content, they don't just stick around. They bring others with them. CLV has a multiplier effect. Loyal users help grow reach organically, pulling their social networks into the fold. Media is, after all, a form of social glue.

The more connected the audience, the more valuable the system. That's how networks grow. That's how hubs form. It's classic preferential attachment: people are drawn to what's already popular, already relevant, already "fit" for their needs.

CLV also keeps media companies agile. When your goal is long-term engagement, you can't become complacent. You can't over-monetize or under-deliver. You have to earn attention every single day. That pressure to perform 24–7 forces content teams to stay sharp, consistent, and aligned with what audiences actually want. Because at any time, they can go elsewhere.

It's a self-reinforcing system. Focus on long-term value, and the short-term results often follow. Ignore it, and you risk burning out your audience before they ever get a chance to become loyal.

No One-Size-Fits-All Fix

Audiences are not monoliths. And the path forward won't come from a single solution. If we want to restore a more balanced media ecosystem—one that serves people as well as business models—we need to start by recognizing the diversity of the audience itself. Media strategy must be designed with people in mind. But which people? That's where thoughtful segmentation matters.

Media Generations

Media generations are defined not just by age but by the dominant media environment during their formative years (Block and Schultz 2009). These generational imprints influence how audiences discover, trust, and engage with media across their lives. Each generation has been shaped by the media system they grew up with, and they feel today's strains in different ways.

Older cohorts may remember the Newtonian Media Era, where trusted gatekeepers curated content and mass audiences shared common cultural experiences. They are more likely to feel the loss of media institutions, the erosion of editorial oversight, and the fragmentation of shared narratives. Younger generations, particularly Gen Z, grew up in a radically different landscape. For them, the old norms of mass media never existed. Their formative media experiences have been shaped by algorithmic feeds, personalized content streams, and platform-based identities.

With Gen Z, we have a new problem. As they immerse themselves in social media, they are not just consumers of content; they are also producers and, at times, the product itself. What are the ethics of "audience as ad"? What happens when your cultural worth is tied to your influence—or your willingness to be influenced? These are questions the media industry can no longer afford to ignore.

And to complicate matters further, Gen Z came of age in an era of ad-free streaming services. They watched Netflix and Disney+ without ads and they listened to music on Spotify Premium (because the subscription fees for them were so low) and Apple Music without a single interruption. We trained this generation to reject advertising in professionally curated media environments. Will they ever accept advertising that isn't generated by themselves?

Socioeconomic Segments

Layer on top of this generational divide the increasing inequities of access. In today's subscription-heavy world, media is beginning to mirror broader social divides. Those with disposable income can afford to navigate the Walled Gardens—moving seamlessly between ad-free streaming, curated journalism, and premium experiences. But what's left for those who can't pay to avoid ads? Free content isn't really free. Instead, these platforms rely on aggressive monetization strategies. Are these audiences receiving the same quality of information, entertainment, or opportunities to participate in civic discourse as those who can afford a different media diet?

Media Personas and Use Cases

Finally, even within similar age or income groups, media use itself varies dramatically. Consider the news enthusiast trying to stay informed as local outlets shutter and national platforms put their best content behind paywalls. Or sports fans who can no longer afford to follow their favorite teams across multiple streaming services. Or the social user who relies on free platforms to connect with friends and culture but is increasingly nudged toward commerce, conflict, and content they didn't ask for.

Media personas matter because the needs, behaviors, and expectations of each user shape how they experience the system. And the media diet you follow may reveal as much about your values, access, and risk exposure as your demographic profile ever could (Malthouse, Franks, and Maslowska 2017).

The bottom line: There is no one-size-fits-all fix. Audiences are diverse. And that's not a problem to be solved; it's a reality to be embraced. If we truly want to adopt a customer-centric approach, we must recognize and design for that diversity. That means understanding generational context, addressing inequities in access, and respecting the different ways people use media to inform, entertain, connect, and express themselves.

In Part III of this book, we turn to solutions. But those solutions will only work if they start with a fundamental principle: media must serve the people who use it—*all* people, across generations, income levels, and interests. If we want a healthy media ecosystem, we must first see the audience in all its complexity and then design with care.

Part III

Clarity on the Horizon

Prelude: What to Expect in Part III

After everything we've uncovered—the transformation of media from analog to digital and the unraveling of business models built for another time—Part III turns the page and asks a powerful question: *What now?*

We've arrived at a crossroads. The industry has evolved, but it hasn't necessarily progressed. In the rush to adapt to new technologies, new players, and new forms of monetization, the media business has lost its center. The sacred relationship between content and audience—the one that gave media its original purpose and value—has been pushed to the margins.

Part III invites us to consider how we might bring it back.

We begin with Chapter 14, which addresses the identity crisis at the heart of the media business. With so many competing interests at play—platforms, marketers, algorithms, and data systems—media has become increasingly difficult to define. This chapter asks: What does media stand for today? And what would it take to restore a clear sense of purpose?

In Chapter 15, we return to the Five Global Truths—not as nostalgia but as tools for reorientation. These foundational principles have always helped explain how media works. Now, they can help us evaluate what needs to change. From open circuits to sustainable value exchange, we explore how these truths can still light the path forward.

Chapter 16 revisits the 3Cs—Content, Channels, and Consumers—with a fresh perspective. In today's media world, attention is the rarest commodity. That means Consumers must come first, and Channels and Content must work together more fluidly to deliver meaningful, measurable, and human-centered experiences. This reordered energy model helps us rethink where the center of gravity in media actually belongs.

Part III doesn't claim to have all the answers. But it gives us a framework to ask better questions—and to reimagine what a healthier, more sustainable media future might look like.

Clarity may not be guaranteed. But it's not out of reach.

14

Fixing Media's Identity Crisis

We've been on this journey for a long time. We left the Newtonian Media World behind and traveled through chaos, guided by the Five Global Truths. And now that we've arrived in this new digital land, what we see is barely recognizable. Was it a faulty compass? No. All the signs pointed us in the right direction. Yet what lies before us hardly resembles the 3Cs of media we knew so well.

What changed? It wasn't just the players, though there are plenty of new ones in the space. It wasn't just technology, though it now wields unprecedented power. It wasn't just the data, though it seems to have become more prized than what it was meant to measure. And it wasn't just the absence of meaningful regulation, though that's certainly part of the story. It was the cumulative effect of all of it and the unsettling sense that those who now shape the media ecosystem may need a refresher on ethics.

We've spent the first two parts of this book uncovering how we got here. But before we can talk about solutions, we must be clear about the problem. Media is suffering from an identity crisis. The very relationship that once gave media its meaning has been stretched, reshaped, and, in many places, lost altogether.

This chapter is not about fixing everything. It's about highlighting what's been distorted. If we want to restore media's sense of purpose, we have to start by reclaiming its foundation and protecting it from the pressures that pulled it off course.

Media Cannot Become a Means to an End for Someone Else

At its core, media is a relationship between Content, Channels, and Consumers—the 3Cs. When that relationship is strong, everyone benefits. That includes other industries that rely on media to serve their interests. But today, that sacred relationship is being exploited. Too often, media is treated as a tool to capture attention for someone else's purpose. Whether it's selling products, feeding algorithms, collecting customer data, or building personal fame, other priorities have taken hold. When that happens, media loses its integrity. And over time, everyone loses.

Throughout this book, we've met the new players in the media space—marketers, retailers, tech giants, among others. Each player taps into the ecosystem to extract audience attention. These players aren't ignoring content. Many invest heavily in it. But the content they create often serves their goals first and the audience's second. Attention becomes something to trap, monetize, and repurpose. Like flypaper. Often, there's little regard for what originally drew the audience in. As long as it did the job.

This shift presents a real danger. When media is reduced to a tool for others' gain, it loses its cultural potency. Its ability to inform, entertain, and connect is hollowed out. What remains is a superficial version of the 3Cs. Content and channels end up serving business interests more than they serve people as individuals, as communities, and as a culture.

Many of these external players have built their own media networks. And while they technically follow the 3Cs—creating content, distributing it through channels, and reaching consumers—we should ask a hard question. Are they nurturing the content-consumer bond? Or are they simply extracting as much value as possible from the attention they capture? When extraction becomes the dominant logic, we lose the essence of what makes media powerful.

Imagine the media ecosystem as a shared well. Industries draw from it to reach audiences, but if they keep taking water—attention—without replenishing what keeps the well full—content and connection—the source will eventually run dry. In today's attention economy, media fuels many sectors. But if those sectors don't give back, the entire system becomes unsustainable.

The challenge isn't to reject media's role in supporting other industries. It's to ensure that media remains anchored in its original purpose: forging a meaningful connection between content and audience. Without that bond, there's no attention to monetize, at least not for long.

Legacy media companies aren't the only players capable of sustaining this connection. But those who enter the media space can only succeed if they think and act like media companies. That means investing in content that serves the audience, not just the bottom line. If they're willing to uphold this standard, their interests will be better served in the long run. Because ultimately, keeping the well full is in everyone's best interest.

The Devices and Technologies Are Simply Enablers

In the previous section, we discussed the risk of media becoming a tool for extracting value for external interests. But media isn't just threatened by outside business interests; technology and platforms, which should serve as enablers within the 3Cs framework, are now wielding disproportionate influence. If we allow technology to take center stage, we risk losing the true essence of media. Yes, the "channel" is crucial. But a channel, alone, is not what media should be.

Throughout media history, every generation has had its technology story. From the printing press onward, each technology transformation has played a pivotal role in shaping how content reaches its audiences. Yet, in the 3Cs framework technology has always been a facilitator, not the focal point. Its purpose is to make the delivery of content more seamless and bring audiences closer to that content. However, today, that balance is shifting. Technologies and platforms, which once acted purely as enablers, are increasingly becoming gatekeepers.

The rise of platforms has been a fundamental part of the structure of digital media, as we explored earlier in this book. They give order to the vast network of nodes and make it possible for audiences to find, engage with, and enjoy content. In a digital media world overflowing with content—where individual nodes of information, entertainment, and social connection abound—platforms serve as crucial hubs that organize and distribute the vast array of digital media available. Without platforms acting as aggregators, the digital landscape would be too chaotic to navigate.

However, as these platforms grow more powerful, they risk becoming overly dominant. When platforms are no longer just facilitators but start determining what content deserves attention, the sacred balance of the 3Cs is disrupted. The audience's relationship with content becomes mediated not by the channel in a neutral sense, but by an algorithm with its own objectives—be they monetization, engagement metrics, or data collection. This is the moment where technology, instead of enhancing our media experience, begins to control it.

Marshall McLuhan's Laws of Media warned us of this problem (McLuhan and McLuhan 1988). McLuhan's insight was that every new technology enhances certain capabilities but also risks reversing into something harmful if pushed too far. Platforms have enhanced access to content. But when these technologies start to dictate rather than facilitate, they reverse their original purpose. What should be an enabler of choice and discovery becomes a gatekeeper of content, narrowing the diversity of media experiences.

At this point, we must remember the transient nature of technology itself. As Moore's Law has shown, technologies continually evolve, and the devices or platforms that dominate today may soon fall to obsolescence (Moore 1965). The same algorithms and technologies that seem unshakable now will likely be replaced by newer innovations in the near future. In this sense, our focus on the technologies of today should remain tempered by the understanding that they too will soon pass.

What remains crucial is that we protect the relationship between content and audience, regardless of which technology is in place to facilitate the relationship. And to do that, we need to advocate for technology as an enabler rather than a gatekeeper. The audience should have the ultimate autonomy in determining which media experiences are best for them.

Data Is a By-Product, Not the Core Product

Technology isn't the only force distorting the media ecosystem. Data, too, has shifted from a diagnostic tool to something far more powerful and potentially more dangerous. Like technology, it was never meant to be the star of the show. Its original role was to quantify and clarify the relationship between content and audience. Yet in today's attention economy, nearly every player treats data as a proprietary asset to be harvested, hoarded, and monetized.

Retailers use it to fuel shopper marketing. Marketers use it to optimize owned channels and build customer relationship management (CRM) systems that personalize communication. Media companies use it to understand their audiences, and they share this data with marketers to help them make more efficient and better targeted advertising buys. Tech platforms use data to power closed loop attribution systems. Even creators depend on it to grow their audiences and maximize their income streams. In isolation, none of this is inherently problematic. Data can help inform smarter decisions across the entire media value chain.

The problem is that data is no longer seen as a by-product of audience engagement; it's become the goal itself. Every audience action within and across digital media now creates a data point, and with that flood of metrics has come a kind of paralysis. No decision is made without it. Every piece of content must prove itself against it. Art is sacrificed in service of science. Content is increasingly engineered to meet the metric rather than meet the audience.

The issue runs deeper when data is walled off. In the Newtonian Media Era, audience measurement was often managed by independent third parties. Ratings, circulation figures, and traffic counts were standardized and made available—at a price, but available, nonetheless. Today, audience data is treated as a source of competitive advantage, with each player guarding their own insights and oftentimes refusing to share. When data becomes a closed system, it stops functioning as a currency. Markets only work when everyone has visibility into the exchange.

Data also distorts the incentive structure. When content is produced solely to perform against a KPI (Key Performance Indicator) rather than to engage, inform, or inspire, it leads to a shallow form of connection. Media becomes a numbers game. Quantity overtakes quality. What gets optimized are impressions, not impact.

None of this means data is the enemy. The opposite is true. The right data—openly shared, contextually understood, and tied to the right metrics—can illuminate patterns, unlock value, and strengthen the entire ecosystem. But data must be put back in its place. It must be accessible, not hoarded. It must serve the content–audience relationship, not define it. And it must be a means to insight and not the end itself.

Without meaningful connection between content and audience, there would be no data to collect, no engagement to measure, and no value to extract. The media ecosystem depends on that relationship. And so does data.

Regulation Needs to Catch Up

While data has become a key driver in the media ecosystem, its unchecked growth has exposed another pressing challenge: the need for effective regulation. As media continues to evolve, so must the frameworks that govern it. Without proper oversight, both data and technology can be exploited in ways that undermine trust, transparency, and fairness. This brings us to the critical role of regulation, which, though well-established for legacy media, has yet to fully adapt to the complexities of the digital landscape.

Legacy media companies have long operated under strict standards of accountability. Whether in broadcast or print, regulations were designed to ensure fair access to media (especially on the electromagnetic spectrum), ethical editorial standards, and consumer protection from deceptive content. These regulations included licensing, clear laws governing editorial practices, and consequences for violations, ensuring that media companies adhered to public interest obligations. The FCC played a critical role in overseeing broadcast media, maintaining fair access to airwaves, while the FTC (Federal Trade Commission) regulated advertising practices and consumer rights protections. Congress also passed legislation to promote media accountability, creating a structured system where breaches could result in fines, suspensions, or revocations of licenses.

However, the digital media world has largely escaped this level of scrutiny and control. Platforms like Facebook, Google, X, and others have woven in and out of the regulatory framework, taking advantage of ambiguities in how digital media is classified. Is it media, or is it communication? This entanglement with "dumb pipe" definitions— treating platforms as neutral conduits rather than responsible curators— has allowed tech giants to evade the level of accountability that legacy media faces. Meanwhile, legacy media continues to operate under rigid regulations, creating an imbalance where one sector is scrutinized while another often operates without sufficient oversight.

The difficulty in regulating digital media lies partly in the lack of understanding about its evolving nature. The lines between content creation, distribution, and communication have blurred. The rapid development of technologies and business models has overwhelmed regulatory bodies like the FCC and FTC, which are built to govern static, legacy forms of media. While there is intent to regulate digital platforms, the sheer scale of content, constant innovation, and monopolistic behaviors have outpaced regulators' abilities to enforce meaningful standards.

Regulatory intervention often comes only after crises have unfolded. For example, it wasn't until the Facebook–Cambridge Analytica scandal—where the personal data of millions was mishandled—that the FTC imposed a $5 billion fine on the company. Similarly, Google's monopolistic practices in search and online advertising have only recently attracted serious regulatory scrutiny, despite years of concerns about its dominance. These cases show that regulators are frequently reactive, stepping in only after significant damage has been done, rather than proactively ensuring a fair and transparent media landscape.

We are now facing a regulatory mess where certain forms of media are held to higher standards than others. Legacy media must follow strict rules, while digital platforms continue to exploit gray areas and, at times, avoid responsibility altogether. The challenge going forward is clear: How do we close this regulatory gap? How do we ensure that all media—whether legacy or digital—is held to appropriate standards of accountability? Regulators must rethink their approach and develop frameworks that can keep pace with the rapid changes in the digital media landscape, ensuring that consumers are protected and that the integrity of media is upheld across all platforms.

We Need to Do the Right Thing

Ethics isn't a new concern in media; it's always been there. We've seen it embedded in editorial standards, content guidelines, and consumer protections. But in today's digital media landscape, ethical considerations are often treated as an afterthought that has become overshadowed by business imperatives, algorithmic logic, and short-term performance metrics. When the focus shifts entirely to capturing attention, maximizing engagement, or monetizing data, it's easy to forget the human beings on the other side of the screen.

Media wields influence. It shapes opinions, informs decisions, and creates cultural meaning. That influence carries weight and, with it, responsibility. Every choice made in the creation, curation, and distribution of content is a value-laden decision. Are we amplifying truth or distorting it? Are we respecting user privacy or exploiting it? Are we building connections or stoking division? The answers to these questions matter not just for audience well-being, but for the long-term health of the media ecosystem.

Doing the right thing means re-centering ethical judgment in media practice. It requires creators, platforms, marketers, and regulators to ask not only "Can we?" but "Should we?" The path to restoring media's identity isn't just technological or regulatory—it's moral. If we want audiences to trust the media they engage with, we must earn that trust through transparency, integrity, and an unwavering commitment to the public good.

Reflecting on Media's Future

As we've explored, media is at a crossroads, grappling with an identity crisis driven by new players, shifting technologies, and the rise of data as a powerful resource. The sacred 3Cs relationship between Content, Channels, and Consumers is under threat. Yet, the future of media remains unwritten, and the challenges we face are not insurmountable.

Each of the issues examined in this chapter—whether it's the dominance of platforms, the valuation of data, or regulatory gaps—points to a single core problem. Media is drifting away from its identity. We've seen how business interests treat media as a means to an end, how technology risks becoming a gatekeeper instead of an enabler, and how data is being elevated from a by-product to a core product. All of these shifts weaken the bond between content and the audience.

To restore clarity, the media ecosystem must return to its foundation: the 3Cs. Business interests must recognize that audience attention only exists because of compelling content and that the relationship between content and audience must come first. Technology should facilitate this relationship, not manipulate or control it. Data, while valuable, must remain a tool that reflects the content–audience connection, not something that distorts it. Further, regulation must catch up to these new realities, ensuring accountability across the media landscape. Finally, doing the right thing should be a mandate.

The future of media depends on respecting this core identity. Media cannot simply be a means to serve external interests. It must remain a space where content creators connect meaningfully with their audiences—a space where stories, ideas, and culture thrive. Only by maintaining this focus on the 3Cs can media survive and flourish in a digital world filled with new challenges.

15

Returning to the Essence of the Five Global Truths

The Five Global Truths were originally conceived as a compass to guide us through the messy transition from the analog to the digital media world. As we explored throughout Part I of this book, they served their purpose. But now, as we turn our attention toward the future, we must ask: Do these truths still hold relevance as we navigate the challenges ahead?

To find out, we need to examine the essence of each truth—the principles that reveal what media can achieve when functioning at their best. These truths may still offer valuable insights, but only if we are willing to assess them honestly. That means letting go of ideas that no longer serve us, especially when holding on might only add to the current disorder.

In this chapter, we'll revisit each of the Five Global Truths and critically evaluate their relevance today. The goal is to determine which ideas remain useful and which may no longer serve us well. By reflecting on their impact, we can decide what to carry forward and what to leave behind as we chart the course ahead.

Global Truth #1: Convergence

Convergence began as a powerful force that broke down the old silos of analog media. For the first time, media companies could become truly transmedia—delivering content across multiple formats and screens. Television stations launched streaming apps, magazines became websites, and newspapers added video and audio to their offerings. It was a moment of unprecedented opportunity: media companies were no longer confined to a single format or channel.

But just as they were figuring out how to navigate this new digital terrain, something else happened. The field didn't just open up for them; it opened up for everyone. Suddenly, media companies weren't just competing with each other. They were contending with tech platforms, creators, brands, retailers, and everyday users who could all behave like media. Convergence didn't just blur the lines between media formats; it erased the boundaries around who gets to be considered "media" in the first place.

For audiences, this explosion of content offered both freedom and fatigue. On one hand, they could access anything, anywhere, anytime—from professional journalism to niche entertainment, all from a single device. On the other hand, the sheer volume of options became overwhelming. Choice fatigue set in, and attention began to fragment across the vast digital ecosystem. In response, audiences increasingly turned to platforms to help them decide. Whether conscious or not, they ceded control to algorithms and recommender systems that filtered the chaos on their behalf.

This is the double-edged sword of Convergence. It democratized media creation and access; but in doing so, it unleashed a flood of content that reshaped the economics of media. Yes, we can organize this content. Platforms like Google have become powerful aggregators. And yes, it can be monetized; but not in the same way, or with the same margins, as before. The business model has shifted, favoring some players while leaving others behind. As attention splinters into countless micro-fragments, the question becomes whether anyone beyond the largest platforms can capture enough attention to sustain a viable media business. Convergence unlocked new possibilities for everyone; but it also left us with a fragmented attention economy that no one fully controls.

Ultimately, the verdict on Convergence belongs to the audience. If this explosion of content delivers what people truly need, when and how they need it, then the abundance may be justified. But if audiences are left wading through low-quality, irrelevant, or overwhelming content, then Convergence hasn't empowered them; it's failed them. The true measure of progress isn't how much content the system can produce, but whether that content serves its purpose.

Global Truth #2: Symbiosis

Thanks to Convergence, any media company can now use any form of digital communication—whether audio, video, image, or text—to tell its stories. As long as the content is digitized, it can travel across digital platforms. This opens the door for rich, transmedia storytelling: the ability to tell parts of the same story across multiple formats and touchpoints. It deepens audience engagement and that's a good thing.

But what happens when the audience wants to engage with the same story across different media companies? Suddenly, that promise becomes harder to fulfill. For a story to follow the audience—or for the audience to follow the story—we need data to travel with it. If data remains siloed, we lose sight of the journey. And first-party data, by definition, is trapped within individual domains.

Ironically, in the analog media world, we had a better grasp on measuring audiences across different destinations within a particular media form. Sure, channels like TV, print, and radio operated in silos; but at least we had independent third-party providers that enabled us to compare reach and behavior within those domains. Today, despite all the technical progress, we're still no closer to a full-picture view of audience behavior across the media ecosystem. In fact, we may be further away. As media companies hoard first-party data, each focused on protecting their own turf, the ability to build holistic audience understanding and serve them with truly collaborative stories erodes.

This is the central dilemma of Symbiosis today. It's not that we lack the tools or talent to tell stories across channels. It's that we lack the infrastructure and incentives to do it together. Unless media companies and the platforms that host them find ways to responsibly share data or support third-party measurement, one of the most powerful capabilities of modern media will be stunted.

But here's the twist: Symbiosis may not need formal collaboration to occur. Thanks to the willingness of audiences to cocreate, remix, and share, stories are already traveling across platforms and formats in ways media companies never fully control. Even if a company curates content in a single form, the audience often makes it transmedia. A quote becomes a meme. A scene becomes a TikTok sound. A podcast becomes a tweet thread. This is Symbiosis from the bottom-up.

As long as social platforms remain open and creators don't lock down participatory use with strict copyright enforcement, the audience will continue stitching content together—whether or not the original producers are involved. In many ways, this is the most powerful form of Symbiosis: emergent, participatory, and audience-driven. The question is no longer whether media companies will enable Symbiosis; but whether they'll keep up with the version that's already happening without them.

Global Truth #3: Circuits

Digital circuits allow content to travel between creators and audiences, across platforms and devices. In theory, they make the media ecosystem open, flexible, and scalable. But in practice, the way these Circuits are built and controlled has introduced new forms of restriction. What should be frictionless paths for connection often become chokepoints, Walled Gardens, or ghost towns.

Over time, we've seen Circuits falter in four distinct ways: some become too big, some too small, others too expensive, and some too polluted to function properly.

Some Circuits have grown so large and consolidated that they distort the open web. Google is the clearest example. It powers the infrastructure for content discovery, advertising, browsers, and devices, effectively controlling how information flows across much of the digital ecosystem. This is far from the original vision of a decentralized internet—a world where anyone could create, distribute, and access content freely. When the vast majority of digital traffic is funneled through a single company, openness is lost. That's why the US government is now pressuring Google to break apart. The circuit has become so powerful that regulators are stepping in.

At the other extreme are Circuits that are too narrow to reach audiences en masse. In some cases, the circuit delivers content that appeals to such a narrow audience that it can't generate the scale needed to survive. These niche offerings wither due to lack of demand. In other cases, the offering may be highly valuable, but access is deliberately restricted to those who can pay for it. The circuit is closed off not by lack of interest, but by affordability. One excludes by limited appeal, the other by design.

Even when open circuits exist, access often comes at a cost. The idea of "free" media has always been a myth—broadcast was paid for by advertisers, not audiences. Today, advertisers are diverting resources away from open media and toward closed ecosystems where outcomes can be tracked more precisely. Owned platforms, commerce ecosystems, and closed-loop environments are winning out. In the process, open circuits become harder to fund.

Some Circuits remain open but have become overrun with harmful content. Social media networks revealed the extraordinary potential of Circuits to move content at scale, empowering everyday users to amplify messages. But they also exposed the dangers of unregulated amplification—spreading misinformation, eroding privacy, and fueling division. Governments are now stepping in. At the time of this writing, TikTok faces potential divestiture or removal from the US market. These once-hopeful Circuits have become too polluted to function in the public interest.

Still, there are signs of revival. Free, ad-supported streaming television (FAST) channels and other tiered media offerings that offer a lower cost to audiences in return for advertising are gaining traction. These models aim to strike a balance—expanding access while maintaining enough revenue to support content creation. But the equilibrium is fragile. Scale, access, and sustainability remain in tension.

That's why we must be especially cautious when media circuits are built primarily to serve commerce. If content exists only to drive transactions, audiences may be diverted before they've had a meaningful media experience. When attention is redirected too quickly—before people are informed, entertained, or inspired—media stops functioning as media. It becomes little more than a tool for conversion.

The truth of Circuits is that they are never static. Their openness, integrity, and accessibility are constantly being challenged. The pendulum may never stop moving, but our responsibility is clear: we must understand the tensions and advocate for Circuits that serve the public good while remaining economically viable.

Global Truth #4: Brands

The sheer volume of content now flooding the media ecosystem has made one truth increasingly obvious: audiences can't make sense of it all on their own. Deciding what to watch, read, or listen to—one piece of content at a time—is exhausting. And yet, someone has to curate the experience. If not the audience, then who?

That responsibility can be fulfilled by media brands that consistently signal quality, relevance, and integrity. Or it can be handed over to the algorithm. But when algorithms replace human editorial judgment, we lose something essential. We lose context, discernment, and the subtle cues that come from brand voice, editorial perspective, and institutional values. The Brand, as a trustmark, matters more than ever. They matter not just for loyalty, but for clarity, safety, and value in an overwhelming content landscape.

When we search for something today, we face a quiet but profound decision: do we accept the AI-generated summary at face value? Or do we dig deeper—asking who produced this, where it came from, and whether the brand behind it is one we trust? In an era where any answer can be constructed by an opaque system, the integrity of the Brand standing behind the content is more critical than ever.

Given how much media has transformed, you might expect that the idea of the "transmedia brand" would have become second nature by now. After all, Convergence made it possible for any media brand to produce and distribute digitized content across video, audio, image, and text formats. So why haven't more media companies embraced brand identities that transcend any single media form?

Instead, many are still branding for the distribution platform itself. Broadcasters created new names for their streaming platforms—Peacock, Max, Hulu—rather than unifying them under a singular brand identity. Even legacy powerhouses like The New York Times now have high-profile products like *The Athletic* or *The Daily*, whose branding can overshadow the parent brand itself. It's a missed opportunity. These brands may grow individually, but they don't necessarily reinforce the core brand that built the audience in the first place.

Ironically, it's the individual personalities who are now creators in the media ecosystem who understood the assignment. A journalist with an established audience like Tucker Carlson, Dan Rather, or Terry Moran can jump from the legacy media channel that once employed them to their own space on a platform like Substack. A TikTok personality like Baylen Dupree can end up with her own show on TLC. These personal brands are far more fluid and they demonstrate a critical truth: if the Brand is strong enough, the audience will follow.

This is where brand strength becomes strategic, not just symbolic. The only way to combat platform dominance is to build a brand with enough meaning, fitness, and preferential attachment that it can thrive both inside and outside of any controlling hub if it chooses to. A strong brand lets you take your audience with you. The jury is still out on whether legacy media companies will master this, but one thing is clear: brand is the antidote to the flood of commoditized content that doesn't deserve our attention.

But will the dominant brands in the media ecosystem come from legacy media companies themselves? Or will the real power reside elsewhere: with the marketers who use content to deepen customer relationships, or the retailers who turn media into commerce engines, or the platforms and devices that now shape the media experience itself? We already see signs that the most powerful brands in media may not be media companies at all.

If media companies hope to remain relevant, they must invest in their brand's meaning that travels across channels and devices, resonates with audiences, and stands for something enduring. Otherwise, they'll be left behind—just one more piece of forgettable content in someone else's feed.

We don't yet know who will win the branding arms race: the content creators, the platforms that distribute them, or the devices that deliver the experience. But a powerful media brand can survive in any of these environments. Why? Because without meaningful, trusted content, the others are just dumb pipes. A strong media brand doesn't just secure its place in the audience's repertoire; it becomes a prized asset for everyone else in the ecosystem. In a world of fragmented Circuits and platform dependency, it's the trusted Brand that maintains its value.

Global Truth #5: Economics

Today, media companies face a delicate balancing act among multiple revenue models: extracting direct payment for content, monetizing the audience's attention to content through advertising, or using content as an incentive in ancillary business models such as commerce. The truth is, no single revenue model provides the perfect solution.

The challenges are clear: audiences are experiencing subscription fatigue, weary of paying for multiple services. Advertising, once a reliable revenue stream, is now threatened by overload, with audiences tuning out, skipping, or actively avoiding ads. Meanwhile, marketers are shifting focus to their own media channels, bypassing traditional ad-supported media altogether. Each of these factors places stress on the funding models that media companies have long relied upon.

And now, media companies face a new pressure—one that's harder to detect but no less urgent. Players from outside the traditional media industry are entering the game, not to build sustainable media businesses but to use content as a catalyst for other economic goals. A retailer might launch a streaming platform to drive commerce. A tech company might offer content to attract users and harvest their data. In these cases, media is simply a means to a different end. The content itself doesn't need to pay for its own creation, because it's subsidized by another line of business.

This has created a complicated tension. On the one hand, these alternative models can introduce innovation and fund content in new ways. But they also risk distorting the core media economy. If too much content is created without regard for its own economic sustainability—if it exists merely to serve another business goal—then we risk undermining the media ecosystem's ability to fund itself on its own terms.

That's why it's so important to preserve the idea of media economics as distinct from other business models. At its best, a healthy media economy creates sustainable value at the intersection of Content, Channel, and Consumer. Each of the 3Cs must contribute to that equation. The content must be worth consuming. The channel must be able to carry and monetize it effectively. And the consumer must find it valuable enough to exchange attention, data, or money. Break that chain, and the system becomes unstable.

The models that endure will be those that maintain a healthy value exchange: where audiences get meaningful content and media companies are fairly compensated to keep delivering it. This balance won't be easy; but it's essential. Because if content becomes only a means to someone else's end, the media ecosystem will erode from within—depleting the very source of value it depends on.

The Five Global Truths Can Guide the Way

The Five Global Truths have served as a compass, guiding us through the tumultuous journey into the digital media world. That part of the journey is complete. We've arrived. But as we've discussed throughout this chapter, the work is far from over. These truths continue to be essential tools to help us navigate the ever-evolving digital media world.

The challenges ahead may not come with simple solutions. The digital media world is complex and full of new obstacles. However, by holding onto these Five Global Truths, we have a reliable framework to guide our decisions and strategies. As we move forward into uncharted territory, the compass may not always point to an easy or obvious path. But with each truth firmly in hand, we can chart a course that ensures the media–audience relationship remains centered and sustainable. The answers may evolve, but the truths remain. And with them, we can confidently travel forward in this new media landscape.

16

Renewed Energy
from the 3Cs

Throughout the journey of *Media: From Chaos to Clarity*, the 3Cs—Content, Consumer, and Channel—have been more than just component parts of a definition of media. They've served as the essential energy source that fuels the entire media ecosystem. It's the powerful combination of these three forces that sparks the magic of media. For years, this framework has guided how we understand the media landscape, helping us make sense of the shifting dynamics of audience engagement, technological advances, and content creation.

But while all three are essential, they've never operated as perfectly balanced forces. There has always been a hierarchy of effects—an implicit ordering shaped by the structure and constraints of the media environment at the time.

Back in the Newtonian Media Era, this hierarchy was clear. Channels came first. At the beginning of the book, we described a "Newtonian" Media World that was dominated by the functionality of a relatively few channels that were unique in their technical capabilities. The structure of the channels dictated the forms of content they could support. The circuits were fixed, and they traveled relatively seamlessly from sender to receiver. Content came next in the formula. Thoughtfully curated for the audience in mind, professional gatekeepers produced and distributed content in packages and schedules to appeal to the wants, needs, and desired experiences of the audience. The audience as the consumer of this content was the recipient. They were the end goal in the 3Cs equation. They weren't the lowest priority. Far from it. Everything pointed toward them. Yet, the systems and structures were such that the channel first led us to a particular form of content which would then be selected by the consumer.

Then, as this analog media world began to change before our eyes, we noticed a profound reordering of the 3Cs. Suddenly, what was first in order became last. Thanks to the force of Convergence, any digital channel had the capacity to carry any digital content. The channels themselves became more interchangeable in the mix. So, what rose to first position? It was content. During this period of transformation, we saw an explosion of content, and audiences could seek out the best content experience for them. All they needed to do was use whatever digital device they had handy to do it. But we soon realized that only truly great content that touched the head and the heart of consumers was meaningful. All the other content that flooded the ecosystem was digital exhaust. However, when that content created a spark, consumers became the critical centerpiece of the three-part equation. They became not only recipients of content but powerful accelerants themselves. They could use any conveniently accessible digital device and share that content across their vast digital networks. It was stunning. The channels were still critically important superhighways. They were open circuits of convenience, speed, and scale.

How would we describe the order of the 3Cs today? That's not an easy answer.

A New Orientation for the 3Cs

We're at an inflection point—a moment when the forces of the digital media economy are placing unprecedented strain on the essential bond between the 3Cs. If that bond breaks, the media ecosystem risks spinning further into chaos.

Let's consider the reality.

The 3Cs ordering most recently described during the early digital explosion—Content, Consumer, Channel—no longer holds up. It doesn't account for the rising strategic power of digital channels. The content boom we've experienced over the past two decades has created overwhelming choice; but it's the channel infrastructure that's powered by smart technologies, audience data, and recommendation systems that makes this complexity navigable. Without intelligent channels to filter, surface, and structure the experience, the digital media world becomes out of reach.

Does this mean we've come full circle? Are we back to the old analog media hierarchy of Channel, Content, Consumer? That's equally problematic. In today's platform-dominated world, channels already wield outsized power. Many now serve competing business interests—building walls and monetizing audience behavior in ways that entrap rather than empower. To place channels back at the top would not restore order; it would accelerate collapse.

So, what's the path forward?

There is only one plausible reordering that honors the essence of the 3Cs and provides a way out of the current dysfunction: put the Consumer first. But this time, we don't propose another linear hierarchy. Instead, we suggest placing Content and Channel on a level plane—interdependent and mutually reinforcing. This is not just a philosophical preference. It is a practical solution.

Consumers in Their Rightful Place

This reordering begins by restoring the primacy of the media–audience relationship by placing the consumer at the center of the system. That's the foundation of true customer centricity. When media companies stop focusing on what they want to push and instead solve for what the audience genuinely needs, everything else becomes clearer. Whether audiences seek to be informed, entertained, connected, or comforted, the content and experiences they choose are driven by those lived realities.

That's the essence of the "S" in the SIVA model: media as a solution. It's not just a matter of strategy; it's a matter of survival in a world where attention must be earned, not assumed. Don Schultz made this case years ago through the SIVA model, calling for a shift from product-push to customer-driven solutions. And frankly, it's about time. Compared to other industries, the media business has been notably slow to catch on.

Critics may argue that the consumer was always central to the 3Cs— and it's true that the original energy formula was designed with the consumer in mind. But over time, that bond has weakened. When content is programmed primarily to serve commercial goals, or channels are engineered to trap users for platform gain, the consumer is no longer in control. They're just along for the ride.

That's why placing the Consumer first is no longer just a philosophical stance; it's a safeguard. It's the only way to protect the integrity of media from becoming a means to someone else's end. By elevating the wants, needs, and lived experiences of the audience and by honoring the choices they make within their media repertoire, we preserve the relationship at the heart of the entire system. Not the desires of marketers. Not the monetization goals of platforms. The Consumer. And here's the good news: when we start with the Consumer, there's still plenty of fuel for other interests. They just need to wait their turn.

But let's not mistake the Consumer for a passive recipient. That shift began when digital media first opened the circuits. Consumers evolved from recipients into accelerants—amplifying content that resonates with both their heads and their hearts. Today, their attention fuels the media economy. Their choices signal value. Their engagement drives distribution. And when they share content, they create new circuits of attention that ripple through vast personal networks at the speed of share. In this way, the Consumer is both the receiver of energy and the current that keeps the entire system in motion.

Content and Channel Work Hand in Hand

With the Consumer as the clear focal point, the remaining two Cs— Content and Channel—now sit on the same plane. Both play critical roles in fueling the media engine. Great content still touches the head and the heart, and it still drives engagement. But in today's world, content alone is not enough to ensure success. The sheer volume of content available is staggering, and even the most compelling stories can get lost in the noise if not paired with the right delivery mechanism.

In the digital age, content must be discoverable, shareable, and adaptable across multiple formats. It needs to meet the consumer where they are, whether that's on a mobile phone during their commute, a smart TV in the living room, or a computer at work. The content that wins is not just high quality; it's also optimized for how, when, and where the audience wants to consume it.

Furthermore, content is now often expected to be interactive, personalized, and dynamic. It's not just about delivering a passive experience; it's about creating opportunities for consumers to engage, react, and even cocreate. It sets the stage for consumers of content to accelerate it at the speed of share. The two go hand in hand.

In parallel, the role of the Channel has evolved significantly. What was once considered a mere tool for consuming and sharing content has transformed into a source of economic and strategic value. Thanks to the rise of data-driven platforms, the Channel now plays a much more active role in the media equation.

Channels have become intelligent systems capable of collecting vast amounts of data on audience behavior, preferences, and engagement. This data provides insights that allow media to refine their strategies and create more meaningful experiences for consumers. In many ways, the Channel has become just as valuable as the content it delivers because it provides the infrastructure for understanding the media–audience relationship in real time.

Moreover, in the digital universe, channels that evolve into hubs are essential to the modern media landscape. These hubs serve as central points that aggregate content and provide the necessary infrastructure for all the digital nodes that exist today. It's basic network science and without these hubs with their fitness and preferential attachment, all that rich content is much more difficult to access.

As channels rise in prominence, we need to keep them in check. If the data they produce becomes too valuable or if the walls they erect to function as hubs become too restrictive, we're in trouble. There's a careful balance to strike here: channels must still function as part of a media mix. Audiences simply do not spend 100 percent of their media diet with a single channel. Channels need to collaborate to survive in chaos. No single channel, regardless of how big a hub it becomes, can or should exist on its own. This delicate balance between boundaries and openness is a constant force that must remain in check for channels to function effectively within the 3Cs paradigm.

The Path Forward

This proposed reordering provides the best path forward for restoring media to its core identity and for abiding by the lessons of the Five Global Truths.

It begins by resolving media's identity crisis by re-centering the bond among the 3Cs and reestablishing the audience as the focal point. By elevating the Consumer to their rightful place, we create a safeguard that keeps the relationship between Content and Channel anchored to audience value. This alignment reinforces the foundational energy that powers the entire system and protects it from being hijacked by external business interests.

Just as importantly, this reordering reflects the interconnected nature of the Five Global Truths. These aren't independent concepts; they work together, much like the 3Cs themselves. Each truth reveals how Consumers engage with media and how Content and Channels operate in tandem to shape that experience. From the fluidity of Convergence to the interoperability of Symbiosis, the openness of Circuits, the trust embedded in Brands, and the reciprocal value exchange in Economics, these truths describe a media system that must be audience-first and structurally aligned. That's precisely what this new hierarchy aims to support.

And this isn't just a model for traditional media companies. Anyone who wants to operate in the media business must embrace the 3Cs and put the audience's needs before their own. That's the baseline requirement for participation in a functioning media ecosystem.

This renewed focus on the 3Cs provides an energy formula for all players navigating today's digital world. Properly balanced and aligned, the combination of Consumer, Content, and Channel has the power to drive growth, engagement, and innovation across the ecosystem.

The future will undoubtedly bring new challenges. But by keeping the Consumer at the forefront—supported by meaningful Content and intelligent Channels—the media industry can evolve with intention and resilience.

As we enter this next phase, the energy generated by the 3Cs will remain the renewable force that powers the media ecosystem. When each component honors the media–audience relationship, the system doesn't just function—it thrives.

Epilogue

As we wrap up *Media from Chaos to Clarity and Back Again*, I'm struck by the journey we've taken together—across the years, through the shift from analog to digital, and around every twist and turn that defines this industry. Whether you've been with us since the first edition or are joining for the first time, thank you for being part of this ongoing exploration. It's been a wild ride, and it's far from over.

The media world we first examined now feels like a distant memory. We are firmly in a digital era, surrounded by new players and platforms and an overabundance of everything except the attention of audiences, which is more valuable than ever. Yet, as much as things have changed, some forces remain constant. The 3Cs continue to define media. It's the interaction among Consumers, Content, and Channels that generates the energy that powers the entire system.

But as we've learned, the journey doesn't end there. We've made it into this new digital world only to discover fresh challenges created by the complexity of the media business itself. Frankly, it would have been easier to end the book after Part I, wrapping up the transition from the analog to digital media world with a neat, satisfying conclusion. But that would have done a disservice to you, the reader. The media world is still messy. And even if we don't have all the answers, the problems need to be named and understood.

That meant reevaluating the very tools and frameworks that shaped this book. While the 3Cs remain the best way to define media and understand its impact, we had to reevaluate their order. We also couldn't continue using the Five Global Truths as a compass unless we were willing to put them to the test. In doing so, we discovered that their essence still holds, and they can still help chart a path forward.

Can everything be fixed? Probably not. I worry that the digital marketplaces where advertising is bought and sold will continue to grow in complexity, possibly reaching a point where they're impossible to explain—even in a book like this. I can only hope the system doesn't collapse under its own weight and that we figure it out before it does.

Where do you fit into all of this? That depends on your role. This book was written for a wide audience: students, professionals, and changemakers across the media ecosystem. Each of you brings a unique perspective. And together, you are the architects of what comes next. I'm just here to live in it, write about it, and offer some perspective along the way.

So, what's next? What will it take to gain true clarity? The honest answer is: time. Only time will tell whether the choices we've made—individually and collectively—lead us to greater clarity or usher in new forms of chaos. In five years or maybe in another edition, we'll look back and ask: Did we get it right?

What I do know is this: we've built a foundation. The lessons we've learned about consumer centricity, about balancing content and channel, and about the evolving dynamics of the media business—they'll serve us well. The journey may be bumpy, but it's one fueled by conviction, curiosity, and, yes, a few "Cs" to keep us grounded.

So, as we step back and let time do its work, I invite you to stay curious. The media world will continue to evolve just as we will. And when the time comes to revisit these ideas again, I hope you'll return to help make sense of it all. Until then, thank you for your trust and your company along the way.

Glossary

3Cs (Channels, Content, Consumers) or 3Cs Energy Formula: An expanded definition of media that acknowledges the interrelationships among content, the channel that delivers it, and the audiences that consume it.

4As (American Association of Advertising Agencies): A leading US trade association supporting advertising agencies through advocacy, talent development, industry standards, and research to advance the interests of marketing and communications professionals.

A. C. Nielsen: A global leader in media audience measurement, best known for providing television ratings and cross-platform metrics across TV, streaming, and other broadcast media that serve as trading currency in the advertising marketplace.

AAM: An industry association that independently verifies circulation and audience data for publishers and advertisers. Formerly known as the Audit Bureau of Circulations (ABC), AAM promotes transparency and accountability in media measurement.

Ad Auctions or Auction Marketplaces: A form of digital advertising buying where advertisers bid on available audience attention in near real time.

Ad Exchange: Digital marketplace where the supply side (publishers) and the demand side (advertisers or their proxies) connect to buy and sell digital ad inventory programmatically, typically through real-time bidding systems.

Ad Fatigue: A condition in which audiences become disengaged or irritated by seeing the same or too many ads, reducing effectiveness and prompting behaviors like skipping, blocking, or tuning out.

Advertiser-Supported Revenue Model: A form of media economics where the media company earns its revenue from the sale of advertising time and/or space to marketers.

Aggregator: A digital intermediary that collects content from multiple sources and organizes it in a way that is easily searchable and accessible to users.

Algorithm: A step-by-step procedure or set of rules—often mathematical or logical in nature—used to solve a problem or perform a task. Algorithms automate decision-making, organize information, and guide user experiences.

Amortization: The process of spreading a cost over time and/or multiple uses. It delivers fixed payments toward a debt (both principle and interest) over a payment schedule.

Analog Media: Media formats without any form of digital encoding. Analog media formats are known for their physical chacteristics without the need to translate into code.

Apocalypse Theory: Framing used to describe early reactions to digital media, marked by predictions that new technologies would completely destroy existing media systems, rather than evolve them.

Artificial Intelligence (AI): Computer systems designed to perform tasks requiring human-like intelligence, such as learning, reasoning, and language processing. In media, AI powers recommendation engines, content creation, and audience targeting.

Attention Economy: Media economics concept that frames audience attention as a highly valuable and limited resource that creates value for any form of media. Without an audience and the attention they pay to certain media, there is no value.

Attribution or Attribution Models: The process of identifying which media exposures contribute to a consumer's behavior—especially conversions like purchases—and assigning credit to those exposures accordingly.

Audience Attention Distribution: The allocation of an audience's fixed amount of attention across various media sources. A function of how one spends their time with media.

Audience Autonomy: A term coined by Professor Philip Napoli to describe the degree to which media audiences have the ability to select media that suits their wants, needs, and desired experiences.

Audience Flow: A media company's ability to manage and retain audience attention by guiding viewers or users across content over time, often through scheduling, sequencing, or algorithmic recommendations.

Audience Fragmentation: The division of media consumption across a growing array of platforms, channels, and formats, making it harder for content to reach large, unified audiences.

Albert Lazlo Barabasi: A physicist and network scientist known for pioneering research on scale-free networks. Author of *Linked: The New Science of Networks*, he popularized network science as a field explaining complex, interconnected systems.

Behavioral Ad Targeting: A digital advertising practice that uses data on a person's past online behaviors—such as website visits, searches, and content interactions. Increases advertising relevance by targeting audience segments based on observed behavior.

Behavioral Data: Media audience measurement that tracks an audience's online behavior.

Big Tech: A term used to describe the largest, most influential technology companies due to their significant control over digital platforms, data, and audience access.

Binge Viewing: The consumption of multiple episodes of a television series or video content in one sitting or over a short period of time, typically enabled by on-demand streaming platforms.

Black Box: A system where inputs and outputs are visible, but the internal processes are hidden or not easily understood.

Bot Traffic: Visits to websites and clicks on digital ads that are not made by human audiences. Instead, the traffic is generated by automated software programs that can mimic human behavior.

Brand: Intangible values associated with a product or service that differentiate it from others in the marketplace. One of the Five Global

Truths that defines successful media as those that deliver a promise to audiences that can transcend any media channel.

Brand Safety: Practices used by advertisers to ensure their ads do not appear alongside harmful content. Protects brand reputation by avoiding content that could damage consumer trust or conflict with brand values, especially in programmatic ad buying.

Brand versus Performance Media (False Binary): Media strategy binary that separates efforts to build brand equity from efforts to deliver an immediate response in terms of clicks or even sales.

Business Model: A strategic approach for how any business creates, delivers, and captures value. It defines who the business is for, what the business delivers, and how it will run succesfully.

CalOPPA (California Online Privacy Protection Act): A California law requiring commercial websites and online services to post a privacy policy disclosing what personal data is collected and how it is used. One of the first US laws mandating transparency in online data collection.

Carpe Technology Diem: A critical phrase describing the tendency to let the technology of the day dictate decisions, often displacing strategic thinking or established wisdom in favor of chasing what's new.

Census-Based Measurement: An audience measurement method that tracks individual audience behavior at a detailed level within a particular platform.

Channel: The technical infrastructure that carries content to the audience (the consumer of content). One of the core pillars of the 3Cs definition of media.

Channel Capacity: The amount of content a media channel can carry or support; in digital environments, capacity is effectively limitless, altering the role of curation and gatekeeping.

Circulation (as relates to print media): The number of physical copies of newspapers and/or magazines that are distributed to audiences.

Circuits: One of the Five Global Truths that describes how digitized content flows across media channels, enabling sharing, remixing, and amplification by audiences.

Click-through Rate (CTR): The percentage of the audience that is exposed to a digital advertisement that actually clicks on it.

Clickbait: A sensationalized or misleading content tactic designed to generate clicks, often prioritizing short-term engagement over trust or substance.

Closed-Loop Attribution: A model in which the impact of advertising on sales can be directly tracked within a single ecosystem—typically made possible by platforms like Amazon that control both media and commerce infrastructure.

Commerce-Driven Revenue Model: A revenue model that is driven by the sale of products and services. Usually entails some form of commission or revenue share back to the originator who sponsored the incentive.

Commodity Content: A form of digital content that is excessively abundant and easily replaceable. It often isn't worth paying for and the only way to earn money from it is through advertising.

Common Currency: An industry-accepted audience measurement or standard that allows for consistent evaluation and comparison of media performance across platforms.

Communications Decency Act (Section 230): A provision of the U.S. Communications Decency Act (1996) that protects online platforms from legal liability for user-generated content, while allowing them to moderate content in good faith.

Complexity Bias: The tendency to assign greater value to complex ideas and systems. If it's complicated, it must be better.

Comscore: A pioneer in digital audience measurement, originally known for tracking website traffic. Today, they are building cross-platform audience measurement through their Total Home Panel.

Consumer (as audience): The person who shows up to watch, read, or listen to any form of media content in order to fulfill their wants and needs and desired experiences. One of the core pillars of the 3Cs definition of media.

Content: The information, entertainment, or experiences delivered to audiences through media channels. Content serves as the primary driver of audience attention and is one of the core pillars of the 3Cs definition of media.

Contextual Advertising or Contextual Ad Targeting: The subject matter serves as a proxy for the target audience. Matches ads to what people are reading or watching, without using personal data.

Convergence: One of the Five Global Truths that describes the merging of channels, content formats, and technologies into a unified digital experience.

Convergence Culture: A term popularized by Professor Henry Jenkins that describes the merger of old media with new. The title of his seminal text that describes how digital technologies shape world building and storytelling that can traverse channels (Jenkins 2006).

Cost Structure: A breakdown of all the fixed and variable costs that a company incurs as part of its business model and how these costs relate to each other.

CPA (Cost-per-Action) or CPC (Cost-per-Click): Media pricing model where the media company is paid a fixed fee for every click or action taken by the audience. Shifts media payment from exposure-based to performance-based, tying costs directly to measurable audience engagement.

CPM (Cost-per-Impression): A media pricing model where advertisers pay a set fee for every 1,000 audience impressions. Measurement and payment that focuses on exposure rather than specific audience actions.

Creator: An individual who produces and shares content—such as videos, blogs, podcasts, or social posts—on digital platforms, often building a personal brand and cultivating a direct audience following.

Creator Economy: A term used to describe the growing segment of the media industry where individual content creators—not traditional media companies—drive audience engagement and revenue.

Cultural Cohesion: The degree to which members of the same culture share the same values, beliefs and experiences.

Cultural Production System: The gatekeepers responsible for producing and distributing content that shapes the values, beliefs, and experiences of a culture. Today's culture production system is composed of both formal agents and local grassroots systems (Jenkins 2006).

Customer Centricity: An orientation to marketing that puts the customer at the center of all strategy and operations rather than the business and the brand. A customer-first approach is the cornerstone of modern Integrated Marketing Communication (IMC).

Customer Data Platform (CDP): A CDP integrates customer activity and data from multiple sources across the customer journey in order to create a comprehensive and unified view of a customer using the company's first-party data.

Customer Journey: The dynamic, nonlinear pathway consumers follow when making a purchase decision—spanning awareness, consideration, purchase, and post-purchase loyalty or advocacy.

Customer Lifetime Value (CLV): The projected revenue a customer will generate over the lifetime of their relationship with a business, minus the costs to acquire and maintain that relationship.

D2C (Direct-to-Consumer): A business model where brands or content owners sell products, services, or content directly to consumers, bypassing traditional intermediaries like retailers or media distributors.

Data Management Platform (DMP): A system that collects and organizes audience data from various sources to create anonymous audience segments used for targeting in programmatic advertising.

Data Monetization: The process of generating revenue by leveraging collected data, through direct sales, licensing, or by using data to enhance advertising, content personalization, or business operations.

Demand-Side Platform (DSP): An automated system advertisers use to define target audiences, set bid prices, and purchase digital ad space across multiple programmatic exchanges. DSPs help to optimize programmatic media buying for efficiency and performance.

Decision Fatigue: When media audiences become overwhelmed by the sheer volume of content choices available, making it difficult to fulfill their underlying wants, needs, or experiences from media—a classic paradox of choice.

Digital Display Ads: A visual advertising format delivered across websites, apps, or digital platforms, typically appearing as banners, pop-ups, or sidebars as content loads or is browsed.

Digital Disruption: The shift caused by digital technology that broke the predictable media system of the Newtonian Media Era.

Digital Immigrant: A person who grew up without digital media and adopted digital practices later in life. Digital immigrants choose how fully they engage, from active assimilation to limited participation.

Digital Media: Any form of media whose content is digitized. Any media channel that can carry digitized content.

Digital Native: A person who grew up in the digital media era. They did not need to learn or assimilate into digital technology.

Direct Response Advertising or Direct Response Economic Model: An advertising model where the advertiser pays the media company if the audience takes a measurable action, such as a click or purchase. Only the portion of the audience that responds to the ad is monetized, rather than the total audience that sees it.

Direct-to-Consumer (D2C) Content Providers: Content creators (often entertainment or sports entities) that bypass traditional distributors and deliver content directly to consumers.

Don Schultz: A professor of integrated marketing communications and widely regarded as the Father of IMC, known for pioneering the discipline and championing customer-centric, data-informed approaches to marketing in the modern media era.

Dual Product Marketplace: A media economic principle, coined by Professor Philip Napoli, stating that media companies produce content (product one) to attract audiences and simultaneously sell that attention (product two) to advertisers.

Dumb Pipe: A type of channel that is "content-agnostic." It bears no influence on the content it carries. Instead, it is simply a neutral carrier.

Earned Media: Unpaid brand exposure generated when others voluntarily talk about, share, or cover a brand. This includes formal media coverage, mentions from nonpaid influencers, and conversations among everyday people.

Economics: One of the Five Global Truths that stresses the necessity of viable, sustainable value exchange across Content, Channels, and Consumers.

Economies of Scale: Cost advantages media companies gain as output or audience size increases.

Evergreen Innovation: A type of innovation that has a lasting effect on society. Once it's adopted, it stays significant throughout society over a long period of time.

Extraction Logic: Leveraging the resources of a company (or ecosystem) to satisfy the goals and aims of another industry without replenishing the resources. Refers to leveraging media for other business aims such as commerce without reinvesting in the media's core product.

Fad: A type of innovation that gains popularity quickly and then loses its appeal just as quickly. It seems to come out of nowhere to become extremely popular. Then, it suddenly loses its popularity and fades away.

FAST (Free, Ad-Supported Television): An emerging form of television distribution in the digital media era that does not require a paid subscription to access the ecosystem. Instead, the platform is free to the audience and fully supported by advertising revenue.

Filter Bubble: A personalized digital environment where algorithms serve content that aligns with a user's existing beliefs or preferences, limiting exposure to diverse viewpoints.

First-Party Cookies: Small pieces of data stored on a user's device by the website they are directly visiting, used to remember preferences, login details, or site activity. Its goal is to enhance the user experience by remembering the user's preferences.

First-Party Data: A form of media audience measurement based upon audience interactions on the site. The data is proprietary to its host and is often not shared with other parties.

Fitness: In network science, fitness describes a node's inherent attractiveness to gain connections based on its qualities or resources, influencing its likelihood of becoming a hub.

Five Global Truths: A framework introduced in this book to describe the forces that are reshaping the media landscape in the digital era. They serve as a five-point compass, with each point individually or in tandem with others explaining how digital media operate today.

Fixed Costs: Expenses that remain constant regardless of scale (e.g., salaries, infrastructure).

Flypaper (as metaphor for attention capture): A metaphor describing media content designed solely to trap and hold attention, regardless of its value or relevance to the consumer.

FOMO (Fear of Missing Out): A psychological response triggered by the perception that others are experiencing something desirable without you. FOMO motivates people to engage with trending content or platforms to avoid feeling left out of shared cultural moments.

Fraud or Ad Fraud: Illegitimate activity in digital advertising where impressions, clicks, or actions are faked—often by bots or deceptive practices—to generate revenue without real audience engagement.

Frenemy: A means of collaboration where the parties are both beneficial and also threats to each other. Used to describe the relationship between media and marketers today.

GDPR (General Data Protection Regulation): EU regulation that governs the collection, use, and protection of personal data. Regulates how companies collect, store, and use consumer data by requiring transparency, consent, and limiting data collection to only what is necessary.

Gatekeepers: A person or entity that controls the flow of information in any form to others who seek access to it.

Google News Showcase: A platform that distributes news content that is licensed from publishers to improve the quality of online news.

Hubs (in network science): In network science, a hub is a highly connected node that serves as a central point within a network.

Hybrid Revenue Model: A means of earning revenue from multiple sources. In the case of media, hybrid revenue usually comes from both audience subscriptions and advertising revenue.

IMC (Integrated Marketing Communications): A customer-centered approach to marketing communication founded by Professor Don Schultz, focused on integrating messages and channels around customer needs and relationships.

Influencer or Influencer Marketing: An individual who shapes opinions or behaviors through the social influence they hold among followers. A newer form of digital marketing where brands rely on third parties to persuade audiences on their behalf.

James Webster: A professor of communication and a leading scholar in media audience research, recognized for his contributions to attention economics and for advancing understanding of how audiences navigate choice and exposure in today's digital media age.

John Wanamaker Quote: A nineteenth-century American retailer known for the famous line capturing advertising's historic measurement challenge: "Half the money I spend on advertising is wasted; the trouble is, I don't know which half."

Laws of Media (McLuhan): McLuhan's explanation for how new technologies cycle through culture. The tetrad suggests technology enhances our abilities, renders an existing technology obsolete, retrieves characteristics from older forms, and reverses into its opposite effect.

Legacy Media: A term used by the author to describe media entities that existed in the Newtonian Media Era, and exist still in today's digital media era.

Licensing: Payment to a creator in exchange for the right to distribute their content on a third-party channel, often for a defined time period and under specific terms such as exclusivity or geographic rights.

Long Tail: A term coined by Chris Anderson to describe the many niche nodes that exist in the digital media ecosystem.

Look-Alike Audience: Audience segmentation technique used to identify additional consumers who most closely match the characteristics of an existing, defined segment.

Made-for-Advertising Websites (MFA): Website that has been developed for the sole purpose of monetizing digital advertising. Oftentimes using sensationalized content to incite "clicks" to digital ads.

Mainstream Innovation: A type of innovation that is first embraced by innovators and early adopters before reaching acceptance among the majority (the mainstream). Over time, this type of innovation will decline in popularity and gradually phase out.

Marginal Costs: The additional costs a business incurs to produce one more unit of output.

Marketing Loss: An economic model where a product or service is intentionally sold at a loss to stimulate demand and generate profits through other products, services, or revenue streams.

Marriage of Mindset and Technology: A framework introduced by the author to predict successful innovation. It requires both technological capability and collective readiness among consumers, media, and other stakeholders such as marketers to embrace and sustain it.

Marshall McLuhan: A Canadian media theorist known for the phrases "the medium is the message" and "the global village," McLuhan examined how media technologies shape perception and society. His Laws of Media explain the four properties of any new technology.

Mass Media or Mass Media Era: Media channels capable of reaching large, diverse audiences. A media era dominated by relatively few channels that reached large audiences and created cultural cohesion. Referred to in the text as the Newtonian Media Era.

Media Economics or Media Economic Forms: A branch of economics focused on how media companies create, capture, and exchange value. Media economic forms describe the funding models—such as advertising, subscription, or hybrid approaches—that sustain content creation and distribution.

Media Ecosystem: The complete network of players that fulfill the 3Cs of media—Content, Channels, and Consumers—and their interconnected relationships within the current media landscape.

Media Experiences: The underlying motivations that drive media consumption behavior. The desired end states we seek from our media consumption. Rooted in Uses and Gratifications theory.

Media Generations or Media Generations Theory: A theory by Professors Don Schultz and Martin Block that defines generational cohorts by the prevailing media and technologies of one's teen years, which leave a lasting imprint on media preferences and behaviors.

Media Marketplace: A structured environment where media buyers and sellers exchange access to audience attention, primarily through the sale of advertising time, space, or content placements.

Media Mix: The combination of media channels used to deliver a marketing message to the intended audience, often balanced across paid, owned, earned, and shared media.

Media Rating Council (MRC): An independent, nonprofit organization that audits and accredits media audience measurement services in the United States. The MRC sets industry standards for validity, reliability, and transparency in media measurement.

Media Repertoire: The set of media channels, platforms, and content sources an individual regularly uses. It reflects habitual patterns of media consumption shaped by personal preferences, routines, and access.

Mediamark Research or MRI-Simmons: A third-party media audience measurement service known for its Survey of the American Consumer and its measurement of media audiences, mainly among magazine media.

Metaverse: A term popularized by Mark Zuckerberg to describe a fully immersive virtual environment where users can engage in a virtual life. It relies upon virtual reality (VR) and augmented reality (AR) to transport users into immersive, new worlds.

MLB Advanced Media (MLBAM): MLB's digital media division, created to manage the league's online content and streaming. It became a pioneer in direct-to-consumer sports delivery.

Moore's Law: In lay terms, Moore's Law suggests that technical capacity will exponentially increase in a relatively short period of time. The author uses this concept to describe the transient nature of technology. It will continue to change and improve.

Phillip Napoli: A leading scholar in media policy and economics, known for his work on the dual product marketplace and the value of audience attention.

Network Resilience: In network science, resilience refers to the ability of a network to remain functional despite the removal or failure of nodes, though failure of hubs causes major disruption.

Network Science: The study of how networks form among individual entities and their connections to others. Helps explain how media systems function as interconnected networks of content, channels, and consumers, with influence shaped by connectivity patterns.

Newtonian Media World: A term framed by the author that draws on the metaphor of Newtonian physics to describe a structured, predictable media environment.

Node: A single point within a network that connects to other points. Nodes are the basic units that form networks. A single media outlet, content creator, or distribution point within the media ecosystem.

Open Web: The portion of the internet that is publicly accessible and not confined within proprietary platforms or Walled Gardens. It includes websites, content, and services that can be freely discovered, linked to, and accessed by any user or search engine.

Opportunities to See (OTS): A media measurement term that estimates how many times an individual has the chance to be exposed to a specific piece of content or advertisement, regardless of whether they actually engage with it.

Owned Media: Any media asset directly controlled by a marketer—such as websites, mobile apps, podcasts, or social media pages.

Paid Media: Any form of advertiser-supported media where a marketer pays a company for time and/or space to place their advertising in front of the media company's audience.

Panel-Based Measurement: A research method that uses a representative sample of individuals or households (a panel) to track media consumption behavior. The data collected is projected to estimate broader audience trends.

Parity Content: A classification of media content with comparable alternatives in the same category. While not perfectly substitutable, this content competes for audience attention within a defined category.

Paywall: A system that restricts access to digital content, making it available only to users who have an active subscription.

Performance Marketing or Performance-Based Advertising Models: A marketing approach focused on short-term, measurable outcomes. Emphasizes efficiency and accountability, often prioritizing quick returns over longer-term brand building.

Persona: A fictional, research-based profile that represents a typical customer or audience segment, including key traits like demographics, psychographics, and behaviors.

PESO: Acronym that stands for Paid Media, Earned Media, Shared Media and Owned Media. These classifications describe "who" controls the messaging and "how" the activity is accounted for based upon the rules of financial accounting.

PESO Riddle: An unsolvable riddle by the author to warn about misusing the principles of PESO, "Pay as little as you can. Own as much of the brand experience as possible. And earn favorable brand mentions in a socially networked world."

Platform: A digital environment that connects users with content, services, or other users. Platforms serve as marketplaces and/or aggregators, organizing access, facilitating transactions, and shaping the flow of information, communication, or commerce.

Precision Targeting: Directing advertising only toward those in the media audience who are identified as having the potential to generate business results. It's the antithesis of mass audience targeting.

Preferential Attachment: The tendency for nodes in a network to connect with already well-connected hubs, reinforcing their dominance.

Premium Content: A classification of media content considered highly valuable, scarce, or distinctive, often commanding greater audience attention and higher market rates. This content is typically differentiated by quality, exclusivity, or cultural significance.

Privacy Sandbox: A set of tools and proposals designed to protect consumer privacy online by limiting personal data sharing while still allowing advertisers to reach audiences in more privacy-friendly ways.

Private Marketplace (PMP): A programmatic advertising environment where premium ad inventory is offered to a select group of advertisers by invitation only, allowing more control over placements, pricing, and audience targeting compared to open exchanges.

Programmatic Advertising: An automated system that uses real-time auctions to buy and sell digital ad space, allowing marketers to bid on individual audience impressions at scale using sophisticated data profiles to improve ad targeting and outcomes.

Programmatic Direct: A type of programmatic advertising where ad space is purchased directly from a publisher at a fixed price, without auctions. Combines automation with guaranteed placements and agreed-upon terms.

Programmatic Supply Chain: The series of intermediaries and technology systems involved in programmatic advertising. Known for its complexity and potential for inefficiencies or hidden costs.

Pure-Play Media Company: Companies that focus solely on content production and distribution and audience engagement as their core business.

Random Network: A network where connections between nodes are made randomly, resulting in a relatively uniform distribution of links.

Ratings (TV): A measurement of the percentage of a total television audience tuned in to a specific program at a given time. Used to gauge a program's popularity and determine its value to advertisers.

Readers Per Copy (RPC): An audience measurement metric that estimates how many people read a single copy of a printed publication. Used to calculate total readership beyond just circulation.

Reciprocal Value Exchange: A concept where both parties receive meaningful value from an interaction. In media, this means audiences get valuable content or services in exchange for their time, attention, data, or payment.

Real-Time Bidding (RTB): An automated auction process where digital ad space is bought and sold in real time, allowing advertisers to bid on individual audience impressions as they become available.

Recommender System or Recommendation System: An algorithm-based tool that suggests content, products, or services to users based on their preferences, behavior, or similarities to others. Commonly used by media platforms to personalize user experiences and keep audiences engaged.

Regulatory Lag: The delay between technological innovation and public policy response.

Retail Media Network (RMN): A retailer's owned media that uses its first-party customer data and content either it produces or acquires to engage its shoppers during the purchase process.

Return on Investment (ROI): A performance metric that evaluates how efficiently and effectively spending toward a particular strategy yields the desired business outcomes.

Revenue Model: The approach any business uses to generate income to fund its operations.

Scale or Scalability: The ability of a business, product, or system to grow its reach or output without a proportional increase in costs.

Scale-Free Network: A network structure where a few highly connected hubs dominate while most nodes have minimal links—common in today's digital media ecosystem.

Screen Democracy or Screen Neutrality: An outcome of Convergence where any digital content can be consumed on any screen, meaning all screens compete equally for audience attention, with no inherent advantage based on device or format.

Second Life: A virtual world launched in 2003 where users, through avatars, could explore digital spaces, create content, socialize, and engage in commerce. Considered an early example of immersive virtual environments and user-driven digital economies.

Second-Price Auction: An auction format where the highest bidder wins but pays the price of the second-highest bid, often with a small increment added. Commonly used in programmatic advertising to encourage truthful bidding and reduce overpayment.

Segmentation, Targeting, and Positioning (STP): A business model framework that divides up a category into smaller groups so that businesses can determine "who" their best customers are based upon "what" they can offer them.

Shared Media: When individuals or companies "share" their owned media assets with each other for mutual benefit.

Shiny Objects: Innovations that are driven by hype more so than clear utility and value.

Shoppable Content: A form of content where the audience can purchase embedded products and services without leaving the page. A user can "click" on an item or a link and make a purchase.

Shopper Marketing: A marketing discipline that focuses on facilitating the sale of goods and services. It tends to focus on the transactional stages of the customer journey and relates to consumers in "shopping mode."

Short-Termism: A business mindset that prioritizes immediate results over long-term brand building, customer relationships, or sustainable growth. Often linked to an overreliance on easily measurable, short-term marketing metrics.

SIVA (Solution, Information, Value, Access): A customer-centered marketing approach coined by Professor Don Schultz. SIVA replaces the 4Ps by focusing on solving customer problems and delivering reciprocal value. S = Solution, I = Information, V = Value, A = Access.

Smart TV: A television with built-in internet connectivity that allows users to stream content, access apps, and browse the internet without needing external devices.

Social Media Network: A digital platform where users create profiles, connect with others, and share content. These networks facilitate social interaction, content sharing, and community building across personal, professional, or interest-based groups.

Speed of Share: A term coined by the author to describe how, in a networked digital media environment, consumers rapidly spread content that resonates with them—amplifying it across their networks at the speed of their internet connection.

Spill: The portion of a media audience that falls outside a marketer's intended target, once accepted as a natural part of mass media buys but now often filtered out through precision targeting.

SS Legacy Media: A metaphor for traditional media companies struggling to stay afloat in the digital era—evoking a slow-moving steamship overwhelmed by rapid change.

Streaming Service: A digital platform that aggregates and delivers audio or video content over the internet in real time. Streaming services offer a mix of original and licensed content, allowing users to access media on demand without downloading.

Subscription Fatigue: A consumer response to the growing number of paid subscription services, where the cost and effort of managing multiple subscriptions leads to frustration, cancellations, or reluctance to sign up for new services.

Subscription Revenue Model: A business model where customers pay a recurring fee—typically monthly or annually—for continued access to a product, service, or content, providing predictable and sustained revenue for companies.

Supply-Side Platform (SSP): An automated system publishers use to manage, price and sell digital advertising time/space across multiple programmatic exchanges. SSPs help publishers to maximize the value of their available digital advertising inventory.

Symbiosis: One of the Five Global Truths that describes channels working together to create richer transmedia experiences where each platform contributes something unique.

Tech Giants: A term used to describe the largest and most influential technology companies that control key digital platforms that have risen in prominence in today's digital landscape.

Third-Party Cookies: Small pieces of data stored on a user's device by a domain other than the website being directly visited. They are commonly used to track user behavior across multiple sites and have become a central point of controversy over consumer privacy online.

Traffic Audit Bureau (TAB): A former US industry organization that audited and verified audience measurement for out-of-home (OOH) media, ensuring standardized and credible data for advertisers and media companies. Now known as Geopath.

Transmedia Brands: A term used by the author to describe a media brand whose promise to its audience transcends any single channel, allowing the brand to thrive regardless of the prevailing communication technology.

Transmedia Storytelling: A storytelling approach described by Professor Henry Jenkins in which each channel delivers a distinct part of the story. Each channel stands on its own, but audiences are rewarded with a richer experience when they engage across multiple channels.

Trustmark (Brand): A brand that earns ongoing trust by consistently delivering on its promise. Over time, the brand itself becomes a reliable symbol customers can count on for consistent performance.

Unique Visitor: A count of individual users who visit a website, with each person counted only once during a set time period, no matter how many times they return.

User-Generated Content (UGC): Content created and published by everyday people that is typically shared on digital platforms such as social media, forums, or review sites.

Uses and Gratifications Theory: A media theory that explains how and why people actively select media to fulfill specific needs, typically categorized as information/education, personal identity, social interaction, and entertainment.

Utility (as applied to platforms): Refers to the classification of a communication technology as providing an essential public service, similar to electricity or water. Utilities are subject to regulatory oversight to ensure fair access, reasonable pricing, and responsible operation in the public interest.

Value Proposition: The core promise a business makes to its customers, explaining the unique benefit it delivers and why people should choose it over alternatives.

Viewability or Viewability Metrics: A measurement standard that tracks whether an ad appeared on a user's screen with the opportunity to be seen by a human. Metrics typically account for the percentage of the ad in view and the length of time it remains visible.

Virtual Reality (VR): An immersive digital experience where users interact with a simulated three-dimensional environment through a device such as glasses or a headset.

Walled Garden: A closed environment where a platform controls all content, user experience, and data, limiting outside access.

What Is Past Is Prologue Theory: The flawed belief that old media protocols and practices can successfully manage digital transformation.

References

Amazon. n.d. "What We Do." *About Amazon.* Accessed July 7, 2025. https://www.aboutamazon.com/what-we-do.

Anderson, Chris. 2006. *The Long Tail: Why the Future of Business Is Selling Less of More.* New York: Hyperion.

Association of National Advertisers. 2023. *ANA Programmatic Media Supply Chain Transparency Study—First Look.* June 19. Accessed November 24, 2024. https://www.ana.net/miccontent/show/id/rr-2023-06-ana-progr ammatic-transparency-first-look.

Barabási, Albert-László. 2014. *Linked: How Everything Is Connected to Everything Else and What It Means for Business, Science, and Everyday Life.* New York: Basic Books.

Bertoni, Steven. 2023. "Top Creators 2023." *Forbes*, September 26, 2023. https://www.forbes.com/sites/stevenbertoni/2023/09/26/top-creat ors-2023/.

Block, Martin P., and Don E. Schultz. 2009. *Media Generations: Media Allocation in a Consumer-Controlled Marketplace.* Worthington, Ohio: Prosper Business Development Corporation.

Calaprice, Alice. 2011. *The Ultimate Quotable Einstein.* Princeton, NJ: Princeton University Press.

Dev, Chekitan S., and Don E. Schultz. 2005. "Simply SIVA." *Marketing Management* 14 (2): 36–41.

Franks, Judy Ungar. 2011. *Media: From Chaos to Clarity.* Chicago: The Marketing Democracy, Ltd.

Franks, Judy Ungar. 2016. "Content Strategy in a Paid/Owned/Earned Media World." In *The New Advertising: Branding, Content, and Consumer Relationships in the Data-Driven Social Media Era*, edited by Ruth E. Brown, Valerie K. Jones, and Ming Wang, 315–52. Santa Barbara, CA: Praeger.

Franks, Judy Ungar, Edward C. Malthouse, and Ewa Maslowska. 2024. "Advertising: A Friend, a Foe, or a Frenemy in Building Healthy Media-Audience Relationships." In *Advances in Advertising Research XIV*, edited by Angeline Vignolles and Martin K. Waiguny, 89–105. Wiesbaden: Springer Gabler.

Google. n.d. "Our Approach." *How Search Works*. Accessed July 3, 2025. https://www.google.com/intl/en_us/search/howsearchworks/our-approach/.

Google. 2025. *Privacy Sandbox*. Last updated March 31, 2025. Accessed July 5, 2025. https://privacysandbox.google.com/overview.

The Guardian. 2012. "The Three Little Pigs Advert." YouTube. https://youtube.com/watch?v=vDGrfhJH1P4.

Hulu. 2009. "Alec in Huluwood." Video advertisement. YouTube. https://youtu.be/TxBSPqJd2_Y?si=fIJk3J7ETo52KrH8.

Jenkins, Henry. 2006. *Convergence Culture: Where Old and New Media Collide*. New York: New York University Press.

Jobs, Steve. 2007. "Keynote Address at the Launch of the iPhone." *MacWorld Conference*, San Francisco, CA.

Johnson, Lauren. 2025. "Amazon's Ad Revenue Was $56 Billion Last Year." *Adweek*, February 7, 2025. Accessed July 7, 2025. https://adweek.com/commerce/amazons-ad-revenue-was-56-billion-last-year/.

Lang, Cady. 2017. "*The Daily Show* Created an Entire Presidential Library Just for Donald Trump's Tweets." *Time*, June 16. Accessed July 7, 2025. https://time.com/4822116/daily-show-donald-trump-presidential-library-tweets/.

Lebow, Sara. 2024. "Retail Media Will Account for Almost a Quarter of All US Media Ad Spend in 2028." *eMarketer*, June 21. Accessed July 7, 2025. https://www.emarketer.com/content/retail-media-account-almost-quarter-of-all-us-media-ad-spend-2028.

Lehrfeld, Rich. 2024. "How Walmart Connect Is Putting Walmart's Purpose in Motion." *Walmart Connect*, April 1. Accessed July 5, 2025. https://corporate.walmart.com/news/2024/04/01/how-walmart-connect-is-putting-walmarts-purpose-in-motion.

Malthouse, Edward C., Judy Franks, and Ewa Maslowska. 2017. "Addressable TV Advertising: The Role of Big Data." In *ESOMAR Big Data World*, 116–25. Brooklyn, NY: ESOMAR.

Malthouse, Edward C., Judy U. Franks, Ewa Masłowska, and Yayu Zhou. 2024. "Managing Advertising and Subscription Fees to Maximize Lifetime Value." *International Journal of Advertising* 44 (4): 674–95. https://doi.org/10.1080/02650487.2024.2403310.

McLuhan, Marshall, and Eric McLuhan. 1988. *Laws of Media: The New Science*. Toronto: University of Toronto Press.

Medill Local News Initiative. 2023. "The Local News Crisis Is Deepening: The Country Has Lost More than a Third of Its Newspapers and Two-Thirds of Its Newspaper Journalists since 2005."

Northwestern University. https://localnewsinitiative.northwestern.edu/posts/2023/06/28/local-news-decline-accelerates/.

Minow, Newton N. 1961. "Television and the Public Interest: An Address to the National Association of Broadcasters." Federal Communications Commission. https://fcc.gov/news-events/blog/2011/05/09/vast-wasteland.

Moore, Gordon E. 1965. "Cramming More Components onto Integrated Circuits." *Electronics* 38 (8): 114–17.

Napoli, Philip M. 2003. *Audience Economics: Media Institutions and the Audience Marketplace.* New York: Columbia University Press.

Nasdaq. 2021. "Walmart and Meredith Corporation Partner to Help Families Answer the Universal Question 'What's for Dinner?'" *Nasdaq*, September 8, 2021. https://nasdaq.com/press-release/walmart-and-meredith-corporation-partner-to-help-families-answer-the-universal.

New York Magazine. n.d. "The Strategist." *New York Magazine.* Accessed July 7, 2025. https://nymag.com/strategist/.

Old Spice. 2010. "The Man Your Man Could Smell Like." Video advertisement. YouTube. https://youtube.com/watch?v=owGykVbfgUE.

Palmer, Shelly. 2022. "It's Baaack!" *Shelly Palmer* (blog), May 11. Accessed July 5, 2025. https://shellypalmer.com/2022/05/its-baaack/.

Peck, Abe, and Edward C. Malthouse, eds. 2010. *Medill on Media Engagement.* Creskill, NJ: Hampton Press.

Perloff, Catherine. 2023. "Only One-Third of Every Programmatic Dollar Reaches End-User, ANA Report Finds." *Adweek*, February 28. https://www.adweek.com/media/only-a-third-of-every-programmatic-dollar-reaches-end-user-ana-report-finds/.

Pew Research Center. 2022. *Journalists Highly Concerned about Misinformation, Future of Press Freedoms.* June 14. Accessed November 24, 2024. https://www.pewresearch.org/journalism/2022/06/14/journalists-highly-concerned-about-misinformation-future-of-press-freedoms/.

Pew Research Center. 2023. *Teens, Social Media and Technology 2023.* December 11. Accessed November 24, 2024. https://www.pewresearch.org/internet/2023/12/11/teens-social-media-and-technology-2023/.

Pritchard, Marc S. 2017. "A Call for Transparency in Digital Advertising." Speech presented at the IAB Annual Leadership Meeting, Hollywood, FL, January 29, 2017. Accessed July 9, 2025. https://youtube.com/watch?v=NEUCOsphoI0.

Rubin, Rebecca. 2023. "Inside 'Barbie's' Pink Publicity Machine: How Warner Bros. Pulled Off the Marketing Campaign of the Year." *Variety*, July 23. https://variety.com/2023/film/news/barbie-movie-marketing-campaign-warner-bros-1235677890/.

Safane, Jake. 2024. "The Average Consumer Pays Nearly $1,000 a Year for Subscriptions." *Yahoo Finance*, March 7. Accessed July 10, 2025. https://finance.yahoo.com/news/average-consumer-pays-nearly-1-190009 547.html.

Schreurs, Ruben. 2023. "Is Chumbox Economics Feeding the Industry's MFA Problem?" *AdExchanger*, December 6. https://www.adexchanger.com/the-sell-sider/is-chumbox-economics-feeding-the-industrys-mfa-problem/.

U.S. Code. 1996. *47 U.S.C. § 230*. Communications Decency Act. Washington, DC: US Government Publishing Office.

Webster, James G. *The Marketplace of Attention: How Audiences Take Shape in a Digital Age*. Cambridge, MA: MIT Press, 2014.

Wood, Chris. 2023. "Walmart Launches Shoppable Ads on NBCUniversal's Peacock." *MarTech*, November 7. https://martech.org/walmart-launches-shoppable-ads-on-nbcuniversals-peacock/.

Zucker, Jeff. 2008. "Digital Pennies from Analog Dollars Are Web Content Conundrum." *InformationWeek*, March 13. https://www.informationweek.com/it-leadership/digital-pennies-from-analog-dollars-are-web-content-conundrum.

Discussion Guide

Chapter 1

1. Your Definition of Media

   How would you define "media" in your own words? How does your definition compare to the one proposed in the text?

2. Why Channels Alone Aren't Enough

   Why is a focus on channels, alone, no longer sufficient? How would you distinguish what is truly media from what is, otherwise, a communication technology?

3. The Role of Responsibility

   The chapter explains that media companies hold responsibility for the content they produce or distribute, while communication technologies often do not. What are the consequences of this difference—for audiences, for advertisers, and for society?

4. The Term "Dumb Pipe"

   The text uses the actual term "dumb pipe" to describe a channel without content. What does this term convey, and how does it help clarify the boundaries between communication infrastructure and media?

5. Do You Qualify as Media?

   Reflect on your own behaviors through the lens of the 3Cs—Channels, Content, and Consumers. Based on this framework, would you consider yourself a form of media? Why or why not?

Chapter 2

1. What Drives What?

   The story of media evolution involves many players. Emerging technology played a crucial role—but so did audience behavior. While the two are connected, which do you think had a greater impact on transforming the media landscape: technology or audience behavior? Why?

2. Signs of Stress

   The chapter describes a resistance to change as the Newtonian Media World began to break down. What were some early indicators that the system was no longer working? Do you think that resistance limited the potential of today's media landscape? If so, how? Looking ahead, how might we recognize both the early signs of breakdown and the ways industries resist necessary change?

3. The iPhone as a Turning Point

   The chapter points to the launch of the iPhone as a media "tipping point." Why was this moment so pivotal, and do you agree that it marked the beginning of irreversible change?

4. Outdated Labels

   Why do terms like "old versus new media" or "traditional versus digital" persist? In what ways might these labels be misleading or counterproductive in today's fully digital media world?

5. Your Place in the Media Timeline

   Think about your own media upbringing. Were you raised in the Newtonian Media World, the transition era, or the digital media world? How does that influence your expectations of media today?

Chapter 3

1. Global Truth #1: Convergence and Competition

    Convergence blurred the lines between once-distinct media industries, creating both opportunity and unprecedented competition. Has this shift made the media ecosystem healthier—or were we better off when each form of media had its own space?

2. Global Truth #2: Symbiosis or Overload?

    Symbiosis allows stories to expand across channels, with each format contributing something new. But not every situation warrants more. When does transmedia storytelling enhance your experience—and when is a single format enough?

3. Global Truth #3: The Speed of Share

    The truth of Circuits explains how audiences can now accelerate content at incredible speeds. What does it take for you to share media with others? What makes something worth passing along?

4. Global Truth #4: Built to Last?

    The truth of Brands suggests that strong media brands transcend any single distribution channel. What do you think separates a media brand that endures from one that fades when its original channel becomes obsolete?

5. Global Truth #5: How Do You Spend Your Time and Money?

    The Economics truth reminds us that audiences now drive value through their attention and spending. When you consider your own media habits, how do you decide what's worth your time and money? If you were to create five personal rules to guide your choices, what would they be?

Chapter 4

1. Mapping Strengths and Weaknesses across the Ecosystem

   No single form of media in today's digital landscape can do it all. They each have strengths and weaknesses. How would you design a SWOT analysis considering each of the players introduced in the text? What patterns can you observe?

2. What Does Your Media Diet Say About You?

   Thinking of your own media consumption, how do you divide your time among all these different players? Who receives most of your time and attention? What are the lessons learned from your own media diet?

3. When Should Marketers Play Media Maker versus Media Partner?

   Marketers rely upon all forms of media to engage with their customers; yet, they have become media themselves. When does it make sense for marketers to leverage their own media, and when are they better served by collaborating with different players in this landscape?

4. Defining the Competitive Set in a Fragmented World

   How would you define the competition if you were running a legacy media company? Some would argue that focusing on your core competitors is the best strategy for growth. Others would argue that taking a broader view of the battle for audience attention is warranted. Which approach is right and why?

5. Editorial Standards in a Cross-Channel Landscape

   Imagine you are the head of content strategy for a legacy media company, a brand's owned media channel, and a creator account. How would you write a statement of editorial standards to outline the rules and practices that writers and editors follow when creating content? How are these statements similar? In what ways do they differ?

Chapter 5

1. Too Big to Function—or Too Big to Fail?

   Network science tells us that hubs emerge because of fitness and preferential attachment—but what happens when a platform becomes *too* dominant? Critics argue for breaking up powerful platforms, but from a network perspective, can the nodes survive without the hub? Or does unchecked growth ultimately violate the very principles that made the platform successful in the first place?

2. Algorithmic Power: Helpful Guide or Hidden Hazard?

   Platforms do more than connect audiences to content—through recommender systems and the algorithms that underlie them, they decide what gets seen. What are the problems with algorithmic curation, and are there benefits we shouldn't overlook? Are critics being too harsh, or not harsh enough?

3. Rebundling: Back to the Future?

   The more things change, the more they stay the same. Today's rebundling of streaming services and other media offerings echoes the bundled hubs of the analog era. Is bundled media the natural state of the ecosystem? Or can you make a case for healthy, independent media nodes in a digital world?

4. How Platform-Dependent Are You?

   Think about how you access and engage with media in your daily life. How many of your favorite content sources are tied to major platforms? Could you imagine consuming media without them?

5. Platforms or Utilities? Where Do We Draw the Line?

   Some platforms now wield so much power that they resemble utilities. Should they be treated as public goods and regulated accordingly—or are they simply successful businesses operating within a competitive system?

Chapter 6

1. What Happens When We Lose a Common Language?

   In the Newtonian Media Era, third-party measurement created a common standard—a shared language for trading media value. Today, first-party data is privately held and often shielded from outside scrutiny. What do we lose when we no longer measure by a common currency? What kind of marketplace does that create?

2. Is Vertical Integration Reshaping the Rules?

   As first-party data becomes more valuable, media companies are no longer just storytellers—they're also the ones collecting, analyzing, and monetizing audience behavior. What are the risks and rewards when a single company creates, distributes, and measures its own content? Does this vertical integration strengthen the media ecosystem, or does it blur the lines of accountability?

3. Personalization versus Connection

   Some say personalized media better serves the individual, while others argue it weakens our collective cultural experience. What's your perspective? Do the benefits of personalization outweigh the risks of filter bubbles and audience fragmentation?

4. Is Content Now Just Bait?

   The chapter poses an existential question: if first-party data is "digital media's new gold," has content become just a way to mine that gold? How might this mindset shape what gets created—and what gets ignored? Is data-enhanced content better or more transactional?

5. What Does It Mean to Be Known?

   First-party data promises to understand you better than ever—your preferences, habits, even your needs before you voice them. Is that empowering or invasive? How does it affect your sense of privacy, identity, and control as a media consumer?

Chapter 7

1. What's Your Innovation Tolerance?

    Media technology used to be more stable—older generations grew up in an era where dominant formats and platforms lasted for decades. Today, the pace of change is relentless. We all face constant waves of innovation. Reflect on how you personally respond to emerging technology. Are you an early adopter who jumps right in, or do you take a more cautious "wait and see" approach? What factors shape your level of comfort with change?

2. What Should Ethical Innovation Look Like?

    As regulation struggles to keep pace with new technology, many argue that developers should take responsibility for building ethical safeguards into new tools from the start. But what does that actually mean in practice? What kinds of protections, limitations, or guiding principles should be expected of those creating the next generation of media technologies?

3. Is the Physical World Poised for a Comeback?

    Some predict that future generations will rebel against the saturation of digital media and seek out more physical, tactile experiences. Do you agree? Or do you believe we are headed deeper into virtual and automated environments? What might drive this shift either way?

4. Can Social Media Platforms Stand the Test of Time?

    Most social media platforms rise quickly—then lose relevance just as fast. Is this constant turnover inevitable, or is it possible for a platform to evolve and remain relevant across generations? What conditions would a social platform need to meet in order to endure?

5. Constants in a World of Change

    While this chapter focuses on continuous transformation, what remains the same in the media landscape over time? What patterns, needs, or human behaviors do you see enduring—even as technologies evolve? Why is it important to recognize these constants?

Chapter 8

1. Should the Media Be a "For-Profit" Business?

    The US media system is primarily built on commercial foundations, with limited public funding. What are the strengths of this approach—and what might be its limitations? How might a more publicly funded system change the nature of media content and access?

2. How Do Booms and Busts Reshape the Media Marketplace?

    Marketplaces don't operate in a vacuum—they're influenced by broader economic forces like inflation, recessions, or consumer confidence. How do economic booms and downturns affect the media business? What changes when advertisers cut budgets or when consumers tighten spending? How resilient is the media economy to these external shocks?

3. Has the Attention Economy Gone Too Far?

    The media business depends on capturing audience attention—but at what cost? Where is the line between clever content strategy and manipulative design? Have we crossed it? What ethical standards should govern how media companies compete for attention?

4. Do All Media Players Play by the Same Rules?

    Earlier in the book, you explored the rise of new media players—from platforms to creators to marketers. Do they all operate under the same business model assumptions? Why does it matter if some players prioritize profit, others prioritize community, and some blur the line entirely?

5. If You Were Starting a Media Company, Where Would You Begin?

    Imagine you're launching a new media venture. Based on this chapter's frameworks—audience, value proposition, revenue, cost, partnerships, and scalability—which component would you prioritize first? Why? How would your choices shape the rest of your business model?

Chapter 9

1. Who's Responsible?

    Where should the line be drawn in the value exchange between media companies and marketers? What responsibilities should media companies uphold, and what should fall on marketers? Should media companies be held accountable for more than delivering a high-quality, engaged audience and an advertising environment that fosters attention? Why or why not?

2. Retail Partnerships: Smart Strategy or Slippery Slope?

    Should media companies embrace or resist partnerships with retailers in the content-to-commerce model? Is collaboration the best path forward, or does relying on retailers further diminish media's role? Can these partnerships sustain quality content creation—or will they dilute media's integrity?

3. Retail Media: New Revenue or Zero-Sum Game?

    Has the rise of Retail Media Networks created an influx of new advertising revenue into the media economy? Or is spending on these platforms simply cannibalizing the ad dollars that once supported traditional media companies?

4. The Impact of V1.0 to V3.0 Thinking

    How does the shift from attention (V1.0) to actions (V2.0) to transactions (V3.0) affect how we understand marketing's full value? Does content-to-commerce provide a more complete picture of what marketing can achieve—or does it overemphasize conversion at the expense of brand-building and long-term relationships?

5. Do You Want All Your Media to Be Shoppable?

    When is it helpful to be able to shop directly from the content you're consuming? Are there times when it feels distracting or takes away from the experience? Is this about your mindset—like being in the mood to shop—or does it depend on the platform you're using, such as retail sites or social media? How do context and intention shape how you feel about shoppable content?

Chapter 10

1. Should We Mourn the Loss of Mass Media?

    This chapter makes the case that something important was lost when mass media faded—scale, shared culture, and efficient business models. Do you agree with this premise? Why or why not? Has media gotten better, worse, or just different?

2. Be Careful What You Wish For?

    Advertisers used to complain about the "waste" in mass media audiences. Today, they can target precisely who they want—but they've lost the efficient reach that mass media once delivered. Were advertisers better off with broad audiences and some waste, or is the precision of today's fragmented landscape worth the trade-off?

3. What Counts as "Mass" in a Fragmented World?

    Are there still examples of media that feel truly mass today? What makes something a mass experience now—simultaneous viewing, cultural impact, or viral reach? Has the meaning of "mass" shifted from everyone watching the same thing at once to everyone knowing about it eventually?

4. Has Media Power Truly Decentralized?

    In the Newtonian Media Era, power was concentrated in the hands of a few gatekeepers who decided what got published, aired, or broadcast. Today, anyone can publish—but platforms and algorithms still determine what gets seen. Has power actually become more diverse, or has it simply shifted to new gatekeepers? Who really controls what rises to the top?

5. How Do You Experience Media in a Fragmented World?

    Think about your own media habits. Do you feel more connected or more isolated as a media consumer today? Do you ever feel overwhelmed trying to "keep up"? What kinds of content or experiences make you feel most connected to something bigger?

Chapter 11

1. **Has the Relationship Ever Truly Worked?**

    The relationship between media companies and marketers has always involved mutual benefit—but also tension. Some say it used to be healthier and more balanced, while others argue it's always been complicated. What's your take? Was there ever a golden era of cooperation, or has it always been transactional?

2. **What's the Real Source of the Breakdown?**

    The author points to several factors driving the breakdown in the media–marketer relationship: the rise of owned media, the shift to narrow targeting, the demand for attribution and short-term results, and the treatment of advertising as an expense for accounting purposes. Which of these do you think has had the most damaging impact—and why?

3. **How Does Owned Media Fit into Your Media Habits?**

    Think about the last time you used a brand's owned media—maybe a recipe from a food company, a workout from a fitness brand, or a product demo on a brand's YouTube channel. How often do you turn to these kinds of sources instead of traditional media outlets? Do you see branded media as a helpful substitute—or does it feel too promotional? What influences your level of trust in content that comes directly from marketers?

4. **Should Media Be Treated as a Business Expense—or a Brand Asset?**

    Advertising is often accounted for as a short-term expense—but media can also be a long-term investment in brand equity. Should companies reconsider how they value media? What changes when we stop thinking about media as a cost—and start thinking about it as an asset?

5. **How Can We Fix It?**

    If the relationship between marketers and media companies isn't working the way it used to, what needs to change to make it better? Can you come up with five ideas to make the relationship stronger?

Who do you think is most responsible for doing the work—marketers, media companies, or both? Is this a matter of meeting in the middle, or does one side need to shift more than the other?

Chapter 12

1. Why Do Marketplaces Matter So Much?

   Why are functioning marketplaces so important to the media business? What are the risks to the participants in the exchange—and to what they're offering—when marketplaces don't work well?

2. When Did Complex Start to Mean Better?

   The chapter introduces the idea of "complexity bias"—the belief that complicated systems are smarter or more valuable. Why do you think we fall for that? When does complexity serve a purpose, and when does it become a liability?

3. Has Complexity Created a New Class of Gatekeepers?

   As programmatic advertising became more complex, it gave rise to new players—ad tech vendors, consultants, auditors, and platform specialists. Have these intermediaries helped improve the system, or just added more layers? Who holds the power—and who should be held accountable—when the system doesn't work as intended?

4. Should Media Marketplaces Be Regulated Like Financial Markets?

   The chapter draws a parallel between stock exchanges and programmatic ad markets. Do you agree with the comparison? What lessons could be applied from regulated financial markets to digital advertising? Would more structure and oversight improve the system—or slow it down?

5. Can You Explain It Simply?

   Einstein said, "If you can't explain it simply, you don't understand it well enough." After reading this chapter, how would you explain programmatic advertising to someone new to media? What parts make sense to you—and where do you still feel lost?

Chapter 13

1. Where Would You Start to Fix the Media–Audience Relationship?

   This chapter outlines how each part of the SIVA framework—Solution, Information, Value, and Access—is showing signs of strain. If you had to focus on just one of these dimensions, which would you prioritize and why? What steps might help improve that part of the audience experience?

2. What Are the Ethical Boundaries in Today's Media Ecosystem?

   The chapter raises important questions about fairness and responsibility. As media becomes more dependent on subscriptions and data-driven monetization, are all audiences being treated equally? Do aggressive monetization strategies create a two-tiered system—one for those who can pay to avoid ads and one for those who can't? Where should media companies draw the line between sustainable business models and ethical treatment of their audiences?

3. What Would It Take to Build Audience Loyalty?

   Customer Lifetime Value (CLV) reframes audience relationships as long-term investments rather than short-term transactions. What specific actions could a media company take to build deeper loyalty with its audience? Are there examples you've seen that do this well?

4. How Do Generational Media Habits Shape Expectations?

   The chapter introduces the idea of media generations, especially highlighting Gen Z's experience in a dual system of ad-saturated and ad-free content. How do you think the media environment you grew up with shaped your expectations as an audience member? In what ways are these generational differences creating challenges for media strategy?

5. What Do You Expect from the Media You Use?

   Think about the media you consume every day. What do you expect in return for your time, attention, or money? What makes you stay loyal to a platform—and what prompts you to leave?

Chapter 14

1. When Does Media Lose Its Integrity?

   The chapter argues that media becomes compromised when it is treated merely as a tool for other industries' objectives. In your view, what are the warning signs that a media offering has lost its connection to the audience? How can creators, platforms, and policymakers safeguard the integrity of media experiences?

2. How Should Data Be Used in Service of Media?

   The chapter makes a case for putting data "back in its place." What would a healthy data culture look like in media? How can we ensure that data strengthens the content–audience relationship rather than distorting or replacing it?

3. What Ethical Standards Should Guide the Future of Media?

   Ethics in media have often been secondary to performance and profit. If you could establish one ethical principle that all media players—content creators, platforms, marketers, and regulators—must follow, what would it be and why?

4. What Do You Expect from the Media Relationship—and Is It the Same for Everyone?

   As a consumer, what do you expect from your relationship with media? Do you want to be informed, entertained, inspired—or something else entirely? And do you expect the same kind of relationship from legacy media companies, platforms, influencers, retailers, or marketers? Why might your expectations vary across players?

5. What Should Media's Identity Aspire to Be?

   This chapter argues that media is experiencing an identity crisis—drifting away from its original purpose as a space for meaningful connection between content and audience. If you were to define media's ideal persona, what traits, values, or behaviors would it embody? How would this version of media behave in service of the public good?

Chapter 15

1. Which of the Five Global Truths is most at risk today—and why?

    Each truth—Convergence, Symbiosis, Circuits, Brands, and Economics—plays a critical role in keeping the media ecosystem functional. But the system is fragile. Choose the truth you believe is under the greatest threat right now. What forces are putting it at risk, and what are the consequences if we fail to protect or repair it?

2. Pick your favorite media company and analyze it through the lens of the Five Global Truths.

    Apply the Five Global Truths to a media brand you admire—or one you know well. Do you see evidence that the company is acting on all five? Where are they strongest? Where do they fall short? Use the framework to diagnose how well they're navigating the current media environment.

3. How can the Five Global Truths help us build the ideal media company?

    Imagine you're building a media company from the ground up. How would each truth inform your decisions about content, channel strategy, business model, and brand development? Where would you start—and what trade-offs might you have to make to stay in balance? Consider how these truths work together to keep the media business both creative and sustainable.

4. How do the truths build upon each other—and what happens when they fall out of sync?

    The Five Global Truths aren't isolated ideas. They work in concert to hold the media ecosystem together. Choose two or more truths and explain how they reinforce one another in a healthy media environment. Then, consider what might happen when those connections weaken or break. What warning signs should we look for?

5. Which truth resonates most with you—and why?

    Whether you're a media consumer, strategist, creator, or critic, one of the Global Truths probably hits closer to home than the others.

Which one stands out for you, and why? What experiences or observations make it feel especially relevant in your personal or professional life?

Chapter 16

1. Can You Describe Your Media Habits Using the 3Cs?

    How does your own media behavior fit the 3Cs hierarchy? Do your needs come first? Or, do you feel that one of the other Cs tends to dominate your behavior? Do you see content and channels on equal footing?

2. If You Graded Media Companies Using the 3Cs, Who Would Pass or Fail?

    Imagine using the newly ordered 3Cs—Consumer, Content, and Channel—as a report card. Which companies or platforms do you think would get high marks? Who might only be passing, and who is failing? Support your answers with specific examples.

3. How Can the 3Cs Help Us Navigate What's Next?

    This chapter presents the 3Cs—Consumer, Content, and Channel—as an energy formula for the future of media. How might this framework help you make sense of emerging technologies, shifting audience behaviors, or new content formats? Choose a current media trend and use the 3Cs to evaluate its potential long-term value.

4. Should Channels Be More Than a Pipe?

    With the Consumer on top, this chapter places Content and Channel on equal footing. But is that a good thing? Should channels continue to grow in power—or would we be better off relegating them to the role of passive distributor? What would we gain or lose if channels were stripped of their ability to shape the media experience?

5. What Laws Would You Create to Protect the 3Cs?

   If you were in charge of designing policies to protect the media ecosystem, what's one law you would create for each of the 3Cs—Consumer, Content, and Channel? Think about what each part of the system needs in order to stay healthy, fair, and effective.

Epilogue

As we come to a close, it's now time to visit the five key questions that this book set out to address:

1. How can we best explain migration from the analog to the digital media world?
2. What does today's digital media world look like? How can we anticipate and explain future shifts?
3. In what ways has chaos reemerged in the media business, and what critical issues must be resolved for a sustainable future?
4. How can the 3Cs and Five Global Truths frameworks be applied to offer fresh perspectives on today's challenges?
5. What role can we each play in advocating for and shaping a healthy and sustainable media future?

Index